Making Sweets Making Sweets

Making Sweets

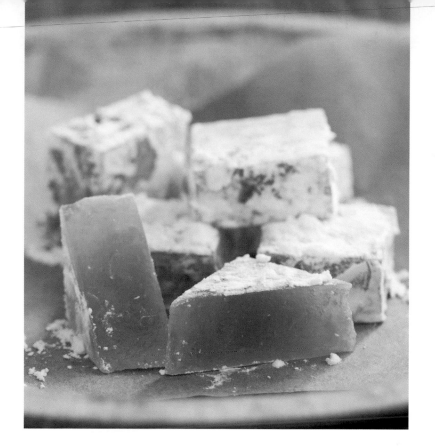

Making
Sweets

A guide to making delicious
confectionery at home

Nina Wanat

APPLE

EDITOR: Beth Sweet

ART DIRECTOR: Kristi Pfeffer

PHOTOGRAPHERS: Diane Cu and Todd Porter

COVER DESIGNER: Amy Sly

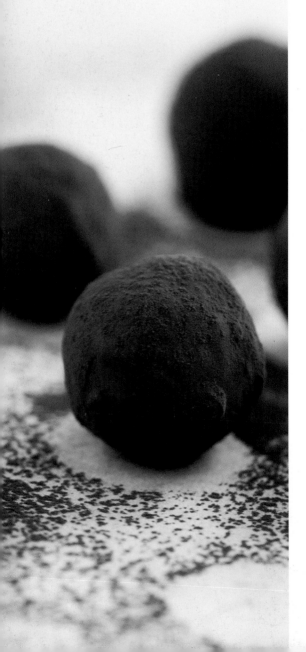

First published in the UK in 2012 by
Apple Press
7 Greenland Street
London NW1 0ND
www.apple-press.com

ISBN 9781 84543 458 8

10 9 8 7 6 5 4 3 2 1

First Edition

Published by Lark Crafts
An Imprint of Sterling Publishing Co., Inc.
387 Park Avenue South, New York, NY 10016

Text © 2011, Nina Wanat
Photography © 2011, Lark Crafts, an Imprint of Sterling Publishing Co., Inc.,
unless otherwise specified

Manufactured in China

Contents

Crunchy Sweets

Chewy Sweets

Silky Sweets

128 In the Pantry

Introduction

Making sweets does not simply make you feel like a kid in a sweet shop – it makes you feel like a kid with *keys* to the sweet shop. You get to enjoy everything about the sweet and unique process, from selecting your favourite flavours, to overseeing the cooking, to sharing your creations with delighted family and friends.

There are tales of wily sweetmakers throughout the ages who kept the secrets of their trade to themselves in order to preserve their mystique and singularity, but I think one of the best-kept secrets is that the sweetmaking process itself is quite a treat. If you've never made sweets before, you will be amazed by the transformation of familiar ingredients – such as sugar, butter and milk – into awe-inspiring confections. There is nothing better than watching an unassumingly transparent sugar syrup whip up into a pristine white billow of marshmallow fluff or witnessing a freshly dipped truffle gradually acquire a firm and glossy shell after being submerged in melted chocolate. If you've previously boiled pots and pots of peanut brittle or devised your own clever version of a nutty chocolate bark, then you are already privy to the magic of the process. And you don't need a fancy commercial kitchen or grandiose appliances to transform your ideas into luscious Pumpkin Caramels (page 70) or decadent Coconut Shells (page 124). This book (and a few basic tools) will have you ready to whip up a batch of deliciousness in no time.

Beautiful sweetmaking is easy and within your reach, and I'm here to guide you through it. No matter how exotic the recipe may seem, sweetmaking can usually be summed up as either a way of boiling and cooling sugar or a way of melting and shaping chocolate. While I am humbly proud of these recipes, I am also a fervent believer that any fresh sweet made with care and good ingredients cannot be beaten, period. Read through the Getting Started section that follows to acquaint (or perhaps re-acquaint!) yourself with the main ingredients, tools and techniques used to make sweets. Then follow any of the recipes in this book, and you'll be rewarded with sweets that taste and look better than anything you can buy.

Beautiful sweets often inspire nostalgic reveries of a holiday or loved one, and the classic, traditional taste of sweets like Toffee (page 38) and Vanilla Marshmallows (page 116) can elicit trips down memory lane. At the same time, sweetmaking is also an exciting way to experiment with new flavours and forms. It's the addition (or sometimes substitution) of an unexpected ingredient that keeps the craft contemporary and exciting. Why not top toffee with smoked almonds instead of roasted almonds? Are you guilty of nibbling away at the dough while baking cookies? Hold the shame, and instead try Chocolate Chip Cookie Dough Fudge (page 100). You know that peanut butter goes well with jelly, but have you ever tasted it with maple syrup in an

"If you've never made sweets before, you will be amazed by the transformation of familiar ingredients – such as sugar, butter and milk – into awe-inspiring confections."

oat-laced Peanut Butter & Maple Praline (page 114)? Timeless tastes, intense flavours and riveting textures – whether they're crunchy, chewy or silky – are the stuff of sweet legends.

There is no better way to treat the tastebuds in your community than to share the sweet rewards of your craft. If you're making a variety of sweets for gifts, part of the fun is thinking about how each confection can stand alone to be admired while at the same time pleasantly complementing all of the others. If, on the other hand, you want to satisfy a single craving, a stylish box filled with uniform, show-stopping sweets is more than a gift – it's a display of skill, care and love.

I hope that this book inspires and delights your sweet-making sensibilities. It is often said that confectionery is based on science and precision, but it is surprisingly flexible to your tastes. I'm confident that some of these recipes will become your family favourites, and it won't be long before you know automatically when to infuse or include your favourite flavours, and when to boil a few degrees higher or lower to suit your preference for texture. Your kitchen and your imagination await – let your creativity and sweet tooth guide you on the satisfying path of crafting beautiful sweets.

Getting Started
Making Sweets

Have you ever noticed how sweet shops, with their gleaming displays of treasures, resemble jewelry shops? Sweets are the most gem-like of foods – vibrantly coloured, exquisitely shaped, dazzling with sparkle or alluring with rich texture.

Making your own sweets may seem exotic or complicated, but, as you'll see once you explore the recipes in this book, most sweetmaking is essentially a matter of boiling and cooling sugar or melting and shaping chocolate. You don't need to be concerned with perfection – they're sweets, have fun! – but because there is some science to the art of sweetmaking, you do need to pay a little more attention to details than usual. If you're new to sweetmaking, familiarise yourself now with the ingredients, tools and techniques I call for in the recipes that follow.

From Top:
Maple syrup, white sugar, honey, brown sugar, corn syrup and molasses; White, milk and dark chocolate; Whipping cream, unsalted butter and whole milk

Ingredients for Sweetmaking

A wide variety of ingredients can be used to make sweets, so be sure to use those that taste the best to you.

SWEETENERS

Granulated sugar is the main building block of sweets. Its neutral flavour and familiar sweetness make it an ideal base for flavours to shine through. Caramelised, its flavour becomes more complex and assertive.

Brown sugar has molasses added back to it after the refining process. It can't be caramelised because of its impurities, but, in traditional recipes, brown sugar is often used to impart a caramel-like flavour to sweets.

Corn syrup is a liquid sugar that imparts sweetness while acting as what's called a "doctor" to prevent crystallization of the granulated sugar in the sweets.

Maple syrup can add wonderful flavour and sweetness to sweets. I recommend using "Grade B" maple syrup, which has a more intense flavour than "Grade A".

Molasses is a by-product of the sugar refining process. The recipes in this book were tested with unsulphured light molasses.

Honey is another source of flavour and sweetness for sweets. I like the neutrally floral flavour of wildflower honey, but if you have your own favourite variety, feel free to try it.

CHOCOLATES

There are so many exciting chocolates available these days. In general, I recommend using blended, neutral-tasting chocolates for sweetmaking, so the chocolate won't overpower or conflict with the filling, but don't be afraid to experiment with whatever you enjoy eating. Callebaut, Valrhona, Scharffenberger, Ghirardelli, and Guittard make good quality chocolate that can be purchased in slab form for sweetmaking.

Chocolate is usually made of cocoa solids (cocoa powder and cocoa butter), sugar, vanilla and lecithin. Cocoa butter is one of the few vegetable fats that is solid at room temperature, so it can also be used as a firming agent in recipes such as nougat.

For dark chocolate, I recommend using bittersweet chocolate with 55 to 65 percent cocoa solids. Milk chocolate should contain about 30 percent cocoa solids. White chocolate does not contain the cocoa powder part of cocoa solids, but it is required to contain at least 20 percent cocoa butter.

Chocolate that's melted for recipes needs to be tempered (see How to Temper Chocolate, page 20). Coating chocolate (also called compound or dipping chocolate) is a convenient option that doesn't contain cocoa butter, so it doesn't need to be tempered. Once melted, coating chocolate is ready to be dipped or moulded. It can be found online, at large craft stores and in the produce section of some grocery stores (since it's used to dip fruits).

DAIRY

Due to its fat content, dairy adds flavour, richness and a distinct texture to sweets. It's important to use unsalted butter, whipping cream and whole milk for the recipes in this book for the proper results. Margarine and low-fat substitutes just won't work in the same ways.

BUTTER & OIL

Butter doesn't need to be at room temperature when used in boiled sweets, such as toffee, but for recipes where it will be mixed in uncooked, such as the Pastel Butter Mints (page 126), it should be softened to room temperature before use.

A neutral oil, such as a canola or vegetable oil, should be used as non-stick agents in pans. Spray oils work well, or you could dab oil on a paper towel to spread in the pan.

Clockwise from top left:
Eggs and cream of tartar;
Rum, bourbon, pear liqueur and tequila;
Hazelnuts, pecans, cashews, walnuts, almonds,
peanuts, pistachios, coconut and macadamias

EGGS

Use large eggs for the recipes in this book, and keep them refrigerated. They don't need to be brought to room temperature when making sweets.

SPICES & SALT

Heat helps to release the flavour of spices, so it's best to make spiced sweets with ground spices that are added at the beginning of cooking. Cinnamon and allspice are especially popular around the winter holidays for their festive, warming flavours that go well with fruits and nuts, while cayenne is especially refreshing during the hotter months. At the base of many delicious sweet recipes is the sweet, light flavour of vanilla: learn to create your own vanilla extract in the book's Pantry section (page 130).

Cream of Tartar: This acidic ingredient helps prevent crystallisation in sweets.

Salt: The recipes in this book were tested with kosher salt. Large-crystal finishing salts are excellent garnishes to enhance the flavours of your sweets. Flaky sea salt, mineral-tinged fleur de sel, earthy pink salt and pungent smoked salt are all good options.

NUTS

Peanuts, almonds, pistachios, pecans, walnuts, coconut, cashews, macadamias and hazelnuts are used in this book. Different types of nuts can be used interchangeably in any of these recipes, depending on your taste preference, and you may also try pine nuts or Brazil nuts. Roasting the nuts is optional, but many people, including me, find that roasting enriches their flavour and makes them crisper. Nuts are best chopped with a chef's knife because a food processor will not cut them evenly. Store nuts in the refrigerator or freezer to keep them tasting fresh longer, and taste them before use to make sure they're not rancid.

ALCOHOL

Bourbon, tequila, pear liqueur and rum are used in this book, and I recommended that you use quality alcohol. Only use alcohol that you enjoy the taste of in your sweets. Spirits can be substituted for one another in recipes if you'd like to create your own flavour profiles, but, in general, try to use young, potent spirits whose flavour will be strong enough to come through the other ingredients.

Tools

Baking Pans. These pans have high sides, and when lined with parchment paper, can be used to pour sweets into to set. The recipes in this book call for 20 x 20-cm (8 x 8-inch) baking pans.

Baking Tray Liners. Parchment paper and non-stick silicone mats are invaluable as non-stick surfaces for sweets. They're interchangeable except that parchment paper can be folded to fit baking pans.

Baking Trays. These usually measure 30 x 46 cm (12 x 18 inches), and their flat surface and low sides are perfect to use for dipped candies. Don't use warped baking trays, or your sweets will also turn out warped.

Bowls. I prefer stainless steel bowls for mixing ingredients and to use as the tops of double boilers. They're light-weight, odour-resistant and sturdy. Glass bowls can be used to melt chocolate in the microwave.

Dipping Forks. Chocolate-dipping forks are available with two or three tines; many find that the three tines offer greater stability. I like to bend the tines up about 45° so that the fork forms a reclined L shape for ease of dipping and holding. If an uneven puddle of chocolate forms under your dipped sweets, the culprit could be the fork – make sure that the tines are perfectly aligned.

Double Boiler. Although you can buy a double boiler pot set, I find that a stainless steel bowl set over a saucepan of water is the best option because it's the easiest set-up for stirring ingredients.

Food-Safe Gloves. Only use gloves that are marked as "food-safe" to handle the sweets as you're cooking (I purchase mine from chemists.) As you wear them, wash and dry them with paper towels as you would your hands. They will keep your hands clean and your sweets sanitary.

Knives. A serrated knife, with large teeth along its edge, is the best option for chopping chocolate. Otherwise, a chef's knife, with a straight edge, can be used to chop nuts, fruit and marshmallows.

Moulds. Chocolate will take on the complexion of a surface it touches; glossy moulds let you form chocolate into interesting shapes with an attractive glossy surface. Chocolate moulds are either lightweight plastic or heavy-duty polycarbonate. Hard sweets moulds are made from silicone, tempered plastic, or metal to withstand heat.

Pastry Brushes. I prefer silicone brushes to bristle brushes because they don't "shed" into the sweets.

Pizza Wheel. This implement is perfect for cutting slabs of sweets quickly.

Ruler or Straightedge. A clean kitchen ruler or straightedge with measurements comes in handy for cutting sweets into straight lines.

Saucepans. Heavyweight stainless steel saucepans are the best for even heat conduction.

Spatulas. Heatproof silicone spatulas are preferred for stirring boiled sugar syrups. They are also perfect for stirring chocolate because they allow you to cleanly scrape the sides of the bowl with their flat but flexible edges. Offset metal spatulas, which have a bend in their oblong stainless steel blades, are preferred for smoothing the tops of warm slabs of sweets.

Stand Mixer. A sturdy 4.5-L (5-quart) stand mixer is required to make marshmallows and nougat. Unfortunately, hand mixers and elbow grease lack the power and speed to aerate sugar properly.

Thermometers. These are crucial for making chocolate and sweets. A chocolate thermometer must give readings between 27°C (80°F) and 49°C (120°F), and either a glass, non-mercury thermometer or a digital, infrared surface thermometer will work well.

For sweetmaking, the thermometer must give readings between 104°C (220°F) and 154°C (310°F). A clip-on candy thermometer should be read at eye level for accurate readings. Its calibration can be checked by immersing it in boiling water to ensure that it reads 100°C (212°F). If the reading is off, get a new one, and keep that adjustment in mind if cooking in the meantime. You can also use digital instant-read thermometers with probes. Never allow the thermometer to touch the bottom of a saucepan while cooking or else the reading will be inaccurate.

Wooden Spoons. These are best to stir hot sweets that are thick and need to be coated, such as Sour Cream Candied Nuts (page 58). They're more rugged than silicone spatulas (and just as heat-resistant), but they don't scrape the bottoms and sides of pots as thoroughly during cooking and so are not preferred for all recipes.

From top left:
Baking pans and baking trays; Parchment paper, silicone mats, and sweets moulds; Stainless steel bowls and glass bowls; Offset metal spatula, silicone spatula, wooden spoon, candy thermometer, chocolate thermometer, pastry brush, knife, dipping forks and pizza cutter.

Below:
Chef's knife (left); Serrated knife (right)

Sweetmaking Techniques

HOW TO TEMPER CHOCOLATE

If you simply melt chocolate, the fat molecules in the cocoa butter will separate, and it will set with unattractive white streaks and a soft, uneven texture. Tempering is a method of heating and cooling chocolate so that the fat crystals re-form and give the chocolate an attractive hard, glossy finish.

The "seeding method" is a quick and easy way to temper chocolate. It is essentially adding reserved pieces of the chopped chocolate (called the seed) into the melting chocolate. As this unmelted chocolate releases its "good" crystals into the melted chocolate, the fat molecules in the melted chocolate reform into the desired configuration, and you have the perfect melted chocolate to make attractive candies.

Plan to temper at least 450 g (1 pound) of chocolate at a time so that you can maintain its temperature with ease. Temper chocolate right before you're going to use it; otherwise, the good crystals will continue to multiply over time, and the chocolate will become too thick and set with a dull, speckled finish. Tempering should be done in a room that's between 18°C (65°F) and 21°C (70°F). If it's much cooler or warmer, the chocolate will either set too slowly or too quickly. You'll need a chocolate thermometer to make sure your melting temperatures are exactly right.

Steps to Temper Chocolate

Chop the chocolate. Use a serrated knife on a sturdy cutting board to cut the chocolate into pieces no larger than 1 cm (½ inch) per side Ⓐ to ensure that the chocolate will melt evenly over low heat. The best way to chop a slab of chocolate with minimal effort is to start chopping diagonally at one corner and shift the slab so that your knife can take on new corners as they form.

Melt two-thirds of the chocolate, reserving one-third as seed chocolate Ⓑ. Dark chocolate should be fully melted to 46°C (115°F), and milk and white chocolates to 44°C (112°F). To use a double boiler, heat the chocolate in a stainless steel bowl set atop a saucepan of barely simmering water. Stir occasionally with a silicone spatula Ⓒ so that the chocolate melts evenly. When fully melted, remove the chocolate from the heat, but let the water continue to simmer so that it can be used to reheat the chocolate later. Be sure to dry the bottom of the bowl with a towel so that water doesn't drip onto your workspace.

To use a microwave, heat the chocolate in a microwave-safe bowl for 30 seconds. Stir, and repeat until half of the chocolate is melted and the bowl feels warm. Adjust the microwave to 50 percent power, and heat in 5- to 10-second intervals until it's fully melted. Stir between each interval.

B

C

D

Seed the chocolate. Reserve one handful of the seed chocolate (the remaining one-third of chopped chocolate) and stir the rest into the bowl of melted chocolate D. Let the chocolate cool down to 34°C (93°F), stirring occasionally. If all of this chocolate seed melts, add in the reserved handful of seed chocolate and let it melt.

Let the chocolate cool down slightly: Stir dark chocolate until it reaches 31°C (88°F). Stir milk or white chocolate until it reaches 30°C (86°F). The seed should now be completely melted, but if any remains, remove it.

Reheat the chocolate. Set the bowl atop the double boiler for 3-second intervals (or heat in the microwave for 3-second intervals at 50 percent power), stirring and checking the temperature, between each interval. Bring the chocolate to its ideal working temperature for dipping or coating (dark chocolate to 32°C/90°F and milk and white chocolates to 31°C/88°F)

Test the chocolate. Dip a piece of parchment paper or a spoon into the chocolate, and set it on the work surface. If the chocolate sets shiny and smooth within 3 to 5 minutes, congratulations! Your chocolate is in good temper and is ready to be used. If it's streaky, try stirring in more chopped chocolate, and testing again in 5 minutes.

Above: Dip a piece of parchment paper into the chocolate to test its temper. The test on the left is streaky and not yet tempered. The test on the right is shiny and smooth and correctly tempered.

Keep the chocolate tempered. Once the chocolate is tempered and at its ideal working temperature, you must use it before it cools and sets. If the chocolate falls four degrees below its ideal working temperature, you can gently reheat it, but don't let it exceed the ideal working temperature. Heat for 3-second intervals, stirring and checking the temperature between each. If the chocolate is in a stainless steel bowl, you can also warm it with a hair dryer or heat gun for 8-second intervals.

If you have leftover tempered chocolate, you can save it for future use by pouring the chocolate out onto parchment paper, letting it set, breaking it into pieces and then storing it in an airtight container. You'll need to temper this chocolate again before using it in recipes calling for tempered chocolate.

HOW TO DIP CANDIES IN CHOCOLATE

Candies dipped in chocolate look beautiful, taste delicious and always impress. In order to achieve flawless results that showcase your hard work, take time to organise your workspace so that dipping can flow smoothly and you can maintain the ideal working temperature for your tempered chocolate. Starting from left to right, place the pan of sweets centres to be dipped, the bowl of tempered chocolate, the bowl of coating ingredients (for hand-rolled sweets), a parchment-lined baking tray to hold the sweets for setting and any garnishes that will be sprinkled on top.

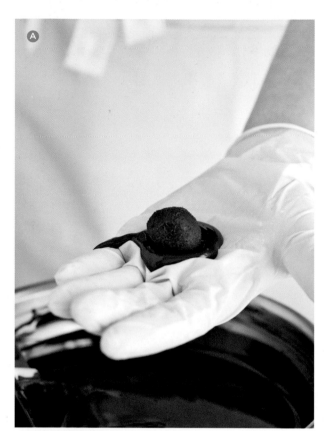

Hand-Rolling Round Candies

It's best to hand-roll round truffles or candies. Put on food-safe gloves, spoon tempered chocolate into the palm of one hand and add the sweet centre . Then roll the sweet and chocolate between your two gloved hands until the sweet centre is completely covered with chocolate B. Roll the covered sweet off your hand and into the bowl of coating ingredients C, such as cocoa powder or powdered sugar. Use a spoon to completely cover the sweet. Continue until the bowl is full of truffles and their coatings have set. Remember to keep a close eye on the temperature of your chocolate to be sure it remains tempered and at ideal working temperature. Use a dipping fork to remove each sweet onto the prepared baking tray.

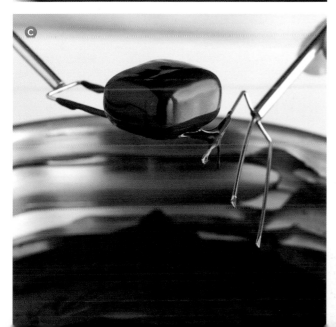

Dipping Rectangular Candies

For rectangular candies, it is best to use two dipping forks, with one in each gloved hand. Place the sweet in the bowl of chocolate, and submerge it with a dipping fork Ⓐ. Slide the dipping fork just halfway underneath the sweet, and lift it out of the chocolate Ⓑ. Move the sweet up and down so that its bottom just touches the top surface of the chocolate. This will help remove excess chocolate from around the piece. Finish the job by scraping the bottom of the sweet with the second dipping fork Ⓒ. Place the sweet on the prepared baking tray by setting down the edge that overhangs the fork first, then lowering the fork and sliding it out from under the piece Ⓓ. Remember to keep a close eye on the temperature of your chocolate to be sure it remains tempered and at ideal working temperature.

E

It's a lot easier to add garnishes to dipped sweets in batches instead of dipping and garnishing one at a time. To do so, start dipping your sweet centres in the chocolate, and keep going until the first one looks slightly matted – now you'll need to stop and add the garnish. Clean your gloved hand of any chocolate residue with a paper towel, and sprinkle or place the garnish onto all of the pieces E. With a second paper towel, clear your dipping forks of any solidified chocolate before continuing to dip.

If your sweet doesn't have a garnish, you can make decorative marks with a dipping fork instead. Wait until the dipped chocolate is just thickening, and press the tines of the dipping fork flat into the chocolate and then pull up and to one side F. You can use three- and two-tine forks to make different patterns that will look beautiful and help identify the flavour.

F

HOW TO COOK SUGAR

Familiar and seemingly unassuming granulated white sugar is the primary structural ingredient of sweets. It's also surprisingly versatile. Sugar can be used to make candies with an infinite variety of textures and flavours. Ending up with the texture and flavour you desire will depend mainly on two things: the temperatures at which you cook and cool the sugar and the procedures you use while cooking. Before you get started, you'll need a good candy thermometer, a clean bowl to hold the finished product and some sugar syrup know-how.

From left: If you stir a boiling sugar syrup that *shouldn't* be stirred, you'll get a pan full of rock hard crystallised sugar. If you don't stir a boiling sugar syrup that *should* be stirred, the syrup will scorch.

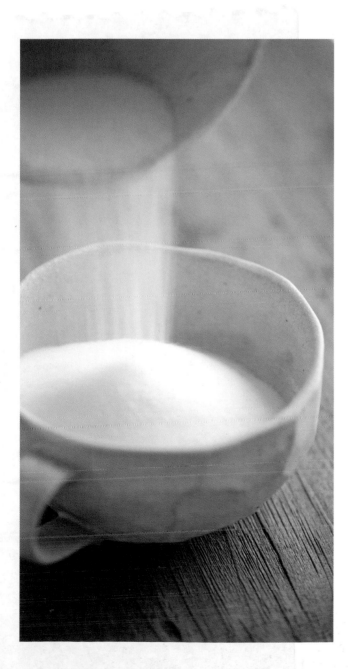

To Stir, or Not to Stir

Most sweets are made by boiling sugar and water into a sugar syrup that's cooked to different stages of firmness. The most important factor during the boiling is whether or not the syrup should be stirred. If you stir a boiling sugar syrup that shouldn't be stirred, the sugar crystals will cling to each other and multiply, leaving you with a saucepan of rock-hard crystallised sugar. On the other hand, if you don't stir a boiling sugar syrup that should be stirred, the syrup will scorch. The recipes in this book will let you know whether or not to stir.

In general, recipes that include butter, cream, or other dairy products need to be stirred while boiling so that the dairy solids cook evenly and don't scorch. The fat in the dairy prevents the sugar from crystallising while being stirred, and the cooking develops the dairy's flavour. You're not stirring to emulsify or mix together ingredients, so it's best to always stir slowly and gently. Keep the spatula in continual contact with the bottom or sides of the saucepan so that the boiling sugar syrup will not splash out – and onto you! If you notice that one area of the saucepan is especially hot and boiling more than the rest of the pan, take care to stir that area frequently. Don't agitate dairy-based candies as they are cooling down, or the fat may separate out of the sweets.

Typically, sugar syrups that don't include dairy (such as those for taffy and hard candies) should not be stirred as they are boiling. However, these sugar syrups do sometimes require agitation as they cool down in order to achieve a certain texture.

Above: Boiling sugar and water into a sugar syrup

How to Cook Sugar Syrup

This is the method to use when water is added to sugar so that it can be cooked to a certain stage of firmness (i.e., soft ball, hard crack). The stages of cooked sugar might seem intimidating at first, but just keep in mind that you're really just boiling the sugar syrup to remove a certain amount of moisture. The longer the syrup boils and the higher the temperature climbs, the more steam escapes the pan and leaves behind a drier and harder sweet.

Begin by pouring water into the pan, and then add the sugar. (The amount of water and sugar added will vary according to the specific recipe you're using.)

Place the pan over the level of heat called for in the recipe, and stir gently until the sugar syrup comes to a rolling boil. Make sure that all of the sugar is dissolved. If crystals of sugar form on the side of the saucepan above the water line, dab them with a wet pastry brush until they are thoroughly dissolved.

After the sugar syrup has come to a boil, clip a candy thermometer on the side of the pan. Don't clip the thermometer on before the syrup boils because sugar crystals may collect around it and remain undissolved.

When the sugar syrup has come to the temperature called for in the recipe, immediately remove the pan from the heat, and pour out the syrup into a clean bowl. Don't scrape the final contents from the bottom of the pan – they're inevitably firmer than the syrup you poured out first.

Tips: *If the temperature of your syrup exceeds the prescribed temperature in the recipe, all is not lost. Simply add a couple of tablespoons of water to the syrup. The temperature will fall, and you can proceed to take it to the correct temperature.*

The best and fastest way to remove cooked sugar from the inside of a pan is to fill it with water and bring it to a boil on the hob. Once the sugar dissolves, wash the pan thoroughly.

1. THREAD 110–112°C (230–234°F)
Syrup forms a thin string.

2. SOFT BALL 113–115.5°C (235–240°F)
Syrup holds its shape as a soft ball for a few seconds.

3. FIRM BALL 116–120.5°C (241–249°F)
Syrup holds its shape as a ball, but is still malleable.

4. HARD BALL 121–131.5°C (250–269°F)
Syrup forms a ball that cannot be flattened.

5. SOFT CRACK 132–143°C (270–290°F)
Syrup holds its shape and bends a little before breaking.

6. HARD CRACK 146–154°C (295–310°F)
Syrup is solid and breaks with pressure.

7. CARAMEL 160–177°C (320–350°F)
Syrup is brown and brittle.

HOW TO CARAMELISE SUGAR

This dry method of caramelisation lets you take a bowl of granulated white sugar and turn it into a saucepan of deep brown liquid caramel without adding any other ingredients. This dry method cooks the sugar so quickly that it cannot be stopped at the various sugar stages, such as soft ball or hard crack. Once sugar is caramelised, it can be stirred without risk of crystallisation because the crystals have already been broken down. It's often then used as an ingredient in sweets, such as chewy caramels, that benefit from its complex dimensions of flavour.

Heat an empty saucepan on medium high for a few minutes.

Pour about a 3-mm (⅛-inch) layer of sugar into the saucepan. If necessary, shake the pan from side to side to get an even layer Ⓐ.

Wherever you first notice a darkened spot of brown caramelised sugar, begin stirring in that spot with a silicone spatula. Gradually swirl the surrounding sugar into the liquefied caramel Ⓑ. At this point, the caramel should still look like a thick tan syrup that's coarse with crystals.

Add another 3-mm (⅛-inch) layer of sugar Ⓒ. Gradually stir it into the caramelised sugar, taking care not to add too much granulated sugar to the caramelised sugar at one time, or it will be too thick to stir. The sugar should stay mostly liquid.

Keep adding layers of sugar one at a time to the saucepan until it is all incorporated Ⓓ.

Stir the sugar so that it cooks evenly until all of the sugar crystals are dissolved and the caramel is amber Ⓔ. You can check for crystals by tilting the pan up and looking for any crystals in the thinnest part of the caramel. The caramel is now ready to be used in your recipe Ⓕ.

GETTING STARTED

Safety Precautions

Boiled sugar syrups can be very hot – sometimes 38°C (100°F) hotter than boiling water – and also very sticky. Always keep a bowl of ice water near you while cooking. If hot sugar splashes onto your hands, immediately plunge them into the water. Do not try to rub hot sugar off with your other hand – it will only stick and burn it, too.

Crunchy Sweets

Toffee

MAKES ABOUT 675 g (*1½ pounds*)

While toffee is a delicious expression of butter, sugar, and salt all on its own, it can be coated with chocolate on one or both sides and have mix-ins in the toffee as well as on the chocolate. You can get creative with digestive biscuits, cookies, nuts, dried fruit, salt or most any other dry food in your cabinets.

METHOD

● Line a baking tray with parchment paper.

● Boil the water, butter, cream, sugar and salt over medium heat in a 3-L (3-quart) saucepan. Stir slowly and constantly with a heatproof spatula until the syrup reaches 149°C (300°F).

● Remove the mixture from the heat, and stir in the vanilla, if using. Pour onto the parchment paper. Let stand 1 minute, then sprinkle chocolate on top of the toffee. Wait 3 to 5 minutes for the chocolate to melt, then spread it evenly over the toffee with an offset spatula. Sprinkle on the almonds, followed by the salt, if using.

● Refrigerate the toffee until the chocolate is set, about 45 minutes. Break into pieces, and store in an airtight container.

VARIATIONS:

Smoked Almond Toffee: Replace the roasted almonds with smoked almonds.

Pistachio & White Chocolate Toffee: Replace the toppings with roasted pistachios, pink Hawaiian salt and white chocolate.

YOU WILL NEED

Baking tray

Parchment paper

3-L (3-quart) saucepan

Heatproof silicone spatula

Candy thermometer

Offset spatula

1   tablespoon water

225 g (8 ounces) butter, cut into cubes

60 ml (¼ cup) cream

200 g (1 cup) sugar

½ teaspoon salt

½ teaspoon vanilla extract (optional) (page 130)

140 g (5 ounces) dark chocolate or coating chocolate, chopped

100 g (1 cup) roasted almonds, chopped (page 134)

Flakey sea salt, for sprinkling (optional)

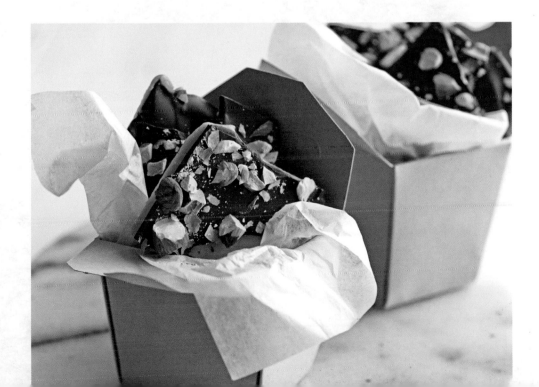

Peanut Brittle

MAKES ABOUT 450 g (1 pound)

Roasted peanuts are the secret to this rich and resonant brittle. Raw peanuts will only toast on the outside during the cooking process, leaving much of their flavour untapped.

YOU WILL NEED

Baking tray

Parchment paper

Pastry brush

Heatproof silicone spatula

Candy thermometer

Offset spatula

60 ml (¼ cup) water

200 g (1 cup) sugar

120 ml (½ cup) corn syrup

150 g (5½ ounces) roasted peanuts (page 134)

3 tablespoons butter

1½ teaspoons kosher salt

¾ teaspoon vanilla extract (page 130)

¾ teaspoon bicarbonate of soda

METHOD

● Line a baking tray with parchment paper.

● Mix together the water, sugar, and corn syrup in a 2-L (2-quart) saucepan until all of the sugar is wet. If sugar crystals cling to the sides of the pan, dissolve them away with a wet pastry brush.

● Bring the mixture to a boil over medium-high heat, stirring occasionally and gently with a heatproof spatula until all of the sugar is dissolved. Then boil to 121°C (250°F) without stirring.

● Add the peanuts and the butter, stirring constantly and gently until the mixture reaches 160°C (320°F).

● Remove from the heat, and stir in the salt, vanilla extract and bicarbonate of soda until thoroughly incorporated.

● Pour the mixture onto the parchment paper, and spread evenly with an offset spatula.

● Let cool completely, about 30 minutes. Break into pieces, and store in an airtight container.

VARIATIONS:
Honey Peanut Brittle: Replace the corn syrup with 75 ml (⅓ cup) honey and 2 tablespoons corn syrup.
Cayenne Peanut Brittle: Add ½ teaspoon cayenne pepper with the peanuts.

Tip: *Use a pastry brush to paint the backs of shards of peanut brittle with tempered chocolate (page 20) or melted chocolate coating for a special treat.*

Rocky Road Chocolate Bark

MAKES ABOUT 675 g (1½ pounds)

I put this recipe in the Crunchy chapter, but the truth is that Rocky Road Chocolate Bark is crunchy, chewy and silky all at the same time! It's also delicious. Once you learn to make this recipe, you'll be ready to experiment with countless chocolate bark variations.

50 g (¾ cup) vanilla marshmallows (page 116), chopped, or 50 g (¾ cup) miniature marshmallows

450 g (1 pound) dark, milk, or white chocolate, tempered (page 20), or 450 g (1 pound) coating chocolate, melted

75 g (¾ cup) almonds, roasted (page 134)

Flakey sea salt or fleur de sel, for sprinkling (optional)

METHOD

● Line a baking tray with parchment paper.

● Scatter the marshmallows onto the parchment paper, over an area of about 25 x 35 cm (10 x 14 inches). Pour on the tempered chocolate, and spread it evenly with an offset spatula. Sprinkle with the almonds and the salt, if using. Let the bark sit undisturbed until set. Break into irregular pieces, and store in an airtight container.

VARIATIONS:

Think of chocolate bark as a blank tablet with endless pages on which to experiment. It's easy to create your own combinations of colours, flavours and textures. Just use the same proportions as in the main recipe and have fun trying different ingredients. Here are a couple of ideas to get you started.

Fruit & Nut Bark: Dark, milk or white chocolate with 75 g (¾ cup) roasted nuts (page 134) and 125 g (¾ cup) dried fruit or crystallised ginger (page 136).

Cookies & Cream Bark: White chocolate with approximately 12 chopped chocolate-and-cream sandwich cookies.

Tips: *If you find yourself with leftover tempered chocolate, use it to make chocolate bark by simply pouring the chocolate onto parchment paper and sprinkling with your favourite toppings.*

Mix ingredients that need to be stored airtight (such as marshmallows and chocolate-and-cream sandwich cookies) into the chocolate rather than sprinkling them on top.

Chocolate-Covered Cereal Clusters

MAKES ABOUT 350 g (¾ pound)

Oh, come on – indulge in a little decadence. Why have cereal in milk when you can eat it in milk chocolate, or even dark chocolate? Crisp, light cereal and a flavourful accompaniment work very well. I suggest cornflakes and raisins, crisped rice and dried tart cherries and oat O's and toffee.

YOU WILL NEED

Baking tray

Parchment paper

Large spoon

Food-safe gloves
or 2 spoons

75 g (¾ cup) cereal

125 g (¾ cup) dried fruit or
toffee, chopped

115 g (4 ounces) dark,
milk or white chocolate,
tempered (page 20), or
chocolate coating, melted

METHOD

● Line a baking tray with parchment paper.

● Mix together all of the ingredients with a large spoon. With gloved hands or two spoons, place small mounds of the mixture on the parchment paper. Work quickly so that the chocolate does not set up in the bowl. Let sit undisturbed until set. Store in an airtight container.

VARIATION:

Peanut Butter & Jelly Clusters: Mix together 140 g (5 ounces) milk chocolate and 55 g (¼ cup) peanut butter. Add 100 g (1 cup) roasted peanuts and 85 g (½ cup) chopped dried (not freeze-dried) strawberries. You'll be amazed by how much this tastes like the sandwich!

Salted Chocolate Caramel Lollipops

MAKES ABOUT 20 lollipops

If you like the delicious combination of salt, chocolate and caramel , you'll love how these lollipops prolong the sensation.

→ YOU WILL NEED

METHOD

● If you don't have lollipop moulds, place a silicone mat on a baking tray.

● Boil the corn syrup, butter, kosher salt and cream in a 1-L (1-quart) saucepan over medium heat. Meanwhile, caramelise the sugar (page 34) over medium-high heat with a heatproof spatula in a 2-L (2-quart) saucepan. When the sugar is caramelised, immediately reduce the heat to low, and add the cream mixture, scraping the pan. Stir over medium-high heat until the mixture is smooth. Add the chocolate. Cook to 134°C (274°F), stirring slowly and constantly.

● Remove from the heat, and quickly drop the syrup from the tip of a large spoon into the cavities of the lollipop moulds, if using. Alternatively, drop the syrup onto the silicone mat so that it forms 5-cm (2-inch) discs, placed to leave space for the sticks. Place a lollipop stick in the centre of each disc, and twist it 180° so that it is fully covered in syrup. Sprinkle the salt on top, crushing it between your fingers so that it's not too jagged. Let cool completely. Peel off the lollipops, and store in an airtight container.

Tip: *If you've got the patience, you can drop the syrup into small dots for free-form boiled sweets instead.*

Lollipop moulds or silicone mat and baking tray

1-L (1-quart) saucepan

Heatproof silicone spatula

2-L (2-quart) saucepan

Candy thermometer

Large spoon

Lollipop sticks

1 tablespoon corn syrup

1 tablespoon butter

¾ teaspoon kosher salt

120 ml (½ cup) cream

200 g (1 cup) sugar

40 g (1½ ounces) chocolate, chopped

Flakey sea salt, for sprinkling

Coffee Lollipops

MAKES ABOUT 16 lollipops

You may feel as if you're experimenting with a chemistry set as you make these irresistible lollipops. The syrup will foam briskly, but all of the bubbles will disappear as it cools to leave you with lollipops as clear as a fresh pot of coffee.

YOU WILL NEED

Lollipop moulds or silicone mat and baking tray

2-L (2-quart) saucepan

Candy thermometer

Heatproof silicone spatula

Large spoon

Lollipop sticks

120 ml (½ cup) coffee

150 g (¾ cup) plus 2 tablespoons sugar

3 tablespoons corn syrup

⅛ teaspoon kosher salt

METHOD

● If you don't have lollipop moulds, place a silicone mat on a baking tray.

● Boil all ingredients over medium heat to 138°C (280°F) in a 2-L (2-quart) saucepan, stirring occasionally with the spatula. Remove from the heat, and quickly drop the syrup from the tip of a large spoon into the cavities of the lollipop moulds, if using. Alternatively, drop the syrup onto the silicone mat so that it forms 5-cm (2-inch) discs, placed to leave space for the sticks. Place a lollipop stick in the centre of each disc, and twist it 180° so that it's fully covered in syrup. Let cool completely. Peel off the lollipops, and store in an airtight container.

Tips: *Don't use parchment paper instead of a silicone mat. If you do, the bubbles in the syrup won't disappear as the sweets sets.*

For a clever gift to a coffee-lover, wrap the tops of the lollipops in cellophane and ribbon, and then present the lollipops in the kind of coffee bag that has a window.

Liquor Lollipops

*MAKES ABOUT **16** lollipops*

While these lollipops are quick to make, you need to wait a day for their flavour to develop – the subtle and intriguing results are worth it. Lollipop moulds make the process quicker, but you can also use a baking tray and silicone mat instead.

METHOD

● If you don't have lollipop moulds, place a silicone mat on a baking tray.

● Mix together 60 ml (¼ cup) of the alcohol, and the water, sugar, corn syrup and salt in a 2-L (2-quart) saucepan until all of the sugar is wet. If sugar crystals cling to the sides of the pan, dissolve them away with a wet pastry brush.

● Bring the mixture to a boil over medium heat, stirring occasionally and gently with a heatproof spatula until all of the sugar is dissolved. Then boil to 149°C (300°F) without stirring.

● Remove from the heat, and mix in the remaining 1 teaspoon alcohol and food colouring, if using. Quickly drop the syrup from the tip of a large spoon into the cavities of the lollipop moulds, if using. Alternatively, drop the syrup onto the silicone mat so that it forms 2-inch discs, placed to leave space for the sticks. Place a lollipop stick in the centre of each disc, and twist it 180° so that it's fully covered in syrup. Let cool completely. Peel off the lollipops, and store in an airtight container.

Tip: *Beautifully presented lollipops in an array of flavours make a creative gift for a spirits aficionado.*

Lollipop moulds or silicone mat and baking tray

2-L (2-quart) saucepan

Pastry brush

Candy thermometer

Heatproof silicone spatula

Large spoon

Lollipop sticks

60 ml (¼ cup) plus 1 teaspoon alcohol, such as bourbon, tequila or rum, divided

2 tablespoons water

150 g (¾ cup) sugar

3 tablespoons corn syrup

⅛ teaspoon kosher salt

¼ teaspoon food colouring of choice (optional)

Honeycomb Sweets

MAKES ABOUT 675 g (*1½ pounds*)

Not only are these sweets a wonder to make because of the way the mixture foams up majestically after the bicarbonate of soda is added, they're also a wonder to eat because of their light, airy crispiness.

→ YOU WILL NEED

Baking tray

Parchment paper

2-L (2-quart) saucepan

Pastry brush

Heatproof silicone spatula

Serrated knife

60 ml (¼ cup) water

200 g (1 cup) sugar

60 ml (¼ cup) corn syrup

2 teaspoons bicarbonate of soda, sifted

900 g (2 pounds) milk or dark chocolate, tempered (page 20), or coating chocolate

METHOD

● Line a baking tray with parchment paper.

● Mix together the water, sugar and corn syrup in a 2-L (2-quart) saucepan without stirring. If sugar crystals cling to the sides of the pan, dissolve them away with a wet pastry brush.

● Boil over medium-high heat without stirring until the syrup just turns golden. Add the bicarbonate of soda. Stir thoroughly and vigorously with a heatproof spatula.

● Pour onto the parchment paper, and let cool without disturbing. Once cool, use a long serrated knife to cut honeycomb into 5-cm (2-inch) long pieces. (It's okay if they're not exactly 2 inches long.) Holding each piece between your thumb and forefinger, dip halfway into the tempered chocolate, letting excess chocolate drip back into the bowl. Place on parchment paper to set, and then store in an airtight container.

Meringues

MAKES ABOUT 60 meringues

I love how the batter for meringues billows up when whisked and then the individual pieces turn crunchy after drying in the oven. You'll love how these meringues dissolve like air on your tongue.

YOU WILL NEED

METHOD

● Preheat the oven to 121°C (250°F).

● Line two baking trays with parchment paper.

● In the bowl of the stand mixer, whisk the egg whites on medium speed until foamy. Add the cream of tartar and salt. Whisk on high speed until soft peaks form. Gradually add the sugar, about a tablespoon at a time, waiting until it's incorporated before adding more. Add the vanilla extract. Whisk until stiff peaks form. Stop whisking, and add food colouring, if using, then mix on low to incorporate.

● Drop the meringue by teaspoonfuls onto the baking trays or pipe small kisses with a pastry bag fitted with a star tip.

● Bake at 121°C (250°F) until dry, 40 to 45 minutes. Let cool before removing from the baking trays.

Tip: *Divide the meringue between different bowls before adding the colouring to make an assortment of different colours from one batch.*

2 baking trays

Parchment paper

5-L (5-quart) stand mixer

Pastry bag (optional)

Star tip for piping (optional)

120 ml (½ cup) egg whites (about 4 large egg whites)

¼ teaspoon cream of tartar

Pinch salt

200 g (1 cup) sugar

1 teaspoon vanilla extract (page 130)

Liquid food colouring, 3 to 5 drops (optional)

Toffee Apples

MAKES 8 apples

Toffee apples can make the unique confectionery claim of being crunchy, chewy and juicy all in the same bite. They're also surprisingly easy and fun to make at home.

METHOD

● Line a baking tray with parchment paper.

● Insert a wooden craft stick into the stem end of each apple.

● Bring the sugar, water and corn syrup to a boil over medium-high heat in a 2-L (2-quart) saucepan, stirring with a heatproof spatula until the sugar dissolves. Then cook to 149°C (300°F) without stirring.

● Remove from the heat, and stir in the cinnamon oil and food colouring, if using. Let the saucepan rest off the heat until the bubbles disappear from the syrup.

● Quickly dip the apples in the syrup, and then swirl gently above the pan so the excess syrup streams off. Place on parchment paper to cool completely.

Tip: *If the syrup gets too thick in the pan, gently reheat it over low heat to thin it out.*

VARIATION:

Spirited Toffee Apples: For toffee apples for adults, decrease the water to 2 tablespoons, and add 1 cup whisky, bourbon or rum with the sugar.

Baking tray

Parchment paper

8 wooden craft sticks

2-L (2-quart) saucepan

Heatproof silicone spatula

Candy thermometer

8   medium apples

600 g (3 cups) sugar

120 ml (½ cup) water

120 ml (½ cup) corn syrup

1   drop cinnamon oil (optional)

1   teaspoon red food colouring (optional)

Sour Cream Candied Nuts

MAKES ABOUT 225 g (2 cups)

This charmingly old-fashioned recipe makes nuts that are enrobed in a thick, sugary coating and infused with an alluring spiciness.

Baking tray

Parchment paper

Wooden spoon

2-quart saucepan

Candy thermometer

Food-safe gloves

100 g (²/₃ cup) packed dark brown sugar

½ teaspoon kosher salt

60 ml (¼ cup) sour cream

¾ teaspoon vanilla extract (page 130)

1½ teaspoons cinnamon

125 g (1¼ cups) walnuts, almonds and/or pecans, roasted (page 134)

METHOD

● Line a baking tray with parchment paper.

● Use a wooden spoon to combine the sugar, salt and sour cream in a 2-L (2-quart) saucepan. Stir occasionally over medium heat until the mixture reaches 115.5°C (240°F).

● Remove from the heat. Add the vanilla, cinnamon and nuts to the syrup, and stir vigorously until the syrup becomes dry and matted, 3 to 5 minutes.

● Pour the coated nuts onto the parchment paper, and immediately separate the nuts using gloved hands. Let cool, and store in an airtight container.

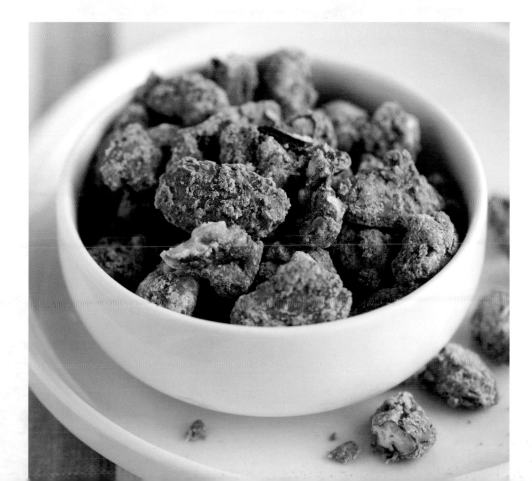

Sweet & Salty Snack Tray

MAKES ENOUGH TO SERVE about 6 snackers

If you're having friends over to watch a big game, this array of treats has it all: salty, sweet, crunchy, spicy and tangy. Individually wrapped in cellophane and presented in a decorative tin, these snacks would also make a much appreciated gift.

METHOD

CHOCOLATE-DIPPED CRISPS AND PRETZELS

● Line a baking tray with parchment paper.

● With gloved hands, dip the crisps halfway in the tempered chocolate, shaking to remove any excess. Place on parchment paper to set. Repeat with the pretzels.

CARAMEL CORN

● Preheat oven to 107°C (225°F). Pour popcorn and roasted nuts, if using, into a roasting pan.

● Combine sugars, water, butter, cream, corn syrup, molasses and salt in a 2-L (2-quart) saucepan. Cook over medium heat, stirring occasionally with a heatproof silicone spatula, until the mixture reaches 121°C (250°F).

(continued)

Baking tray

Parchment paper

Food–safe gloves

Roasting pan

2-L (2-quart) saucepan

Heatproof silicone spatula

Candy thermometer

SOUR CREAM CANDIED NUTS (PAGE 58)

CHOCOLATE-DIPPED CRISPS AND PRETZELS

140 g (5 ounces) ridged potato chips

200 g (7 ounces) thin pretzels

450 g (1 pound) dark or milk chocolate, tempered (page 20)

CARAMEL CORN

300 g (10 cups) popped popcorn, unsalted

100 g (1 cup) roasted nuts, such as peanuts or almonds (page 134)

70 g (½ cup) firmly packed dark brown sugar

100 g (½ cup) sugar

2 tablespoons water

6 tablespoons unsalted butter

2 tablespoons cream

2 tablespoons corn syrup

1 tablespoon molasses

½ teaspoon salt

¼ tsp bicarbonate of soda

● Remove from the heat. Stir in the bicarbonate of soda, and mix thoroughly to incorporate.

● Pour the syrup over the popcorn, and stir until popcorn is coated. Bake for 45 minutes, stirring every 15 minutes. The caramel corn is done when it's dry and crispy when cool. Store in an airtight container.

VARIATION:

Orange Cashew Caramel Corn:
Add 100 g (1 cup) roasted cashews (page 134) to the popcorn, and the zest of 1 orange (1 packed teaspoon) with the cream. Boil to 123°C (254°F) instead of 121°C (250°F). Add 2 teaspoons soy sauce with the bicarbonate of soda.

Above:
Caramel Corn

Below:
Orange Cashew
Caramel Corn

Crystallised Flowers

MAKES 30 pieces

Crystallised flowers are an elegant and edible sweets garnish
for cakes, pastries or truffles.

→

YOU WILL NEED

Whisk

2 small bowls

Small paintbrush

Tweezers

Spoon

Cooling rack

2 egg whites

380 g (2 cups)
caster sugar

30 edible, unsprayed
flowers, such as pansies,
violets or roses

METHOD

● Whisk the egg whites in a small bowl until foamy. Place the sugar
in a small bowl.

● Use a small paintbrush to apply the egg white evenly and
thoroughly onto one flower. Using tweezers, pick up the flower by
its base, and hold it above the bowl of sugar while using a spoon to
sprinkle sugar onto it.

● Place the flower on a cooling rack, and repeat until all flowers
are coated. Let dry completely, at least overnight. Store in an
airtight container.

Tip: *If you don't have caster sugar, you may process granulated
sugar in batches in a clean coffee grinder.*

Chewy Candy

Vanilla Caramels

*MAKES **64** pieces*

These are soft and silky caramels, designed to melt in your mouth while bursting with the full flavors of vanilla and caramel.

YOU WILL NEED

METHOD

● Line an 20 x 20-cm (8 x 8-inch) baking pan with plastic wrap.

● Bring the corn syrup, butter, kosher salt, cream and vanilla seeds and pod to a boil in a 1-L (1-quart) saucepan over medium heat, and then decrease heat to low.

● Meanwhile, caramelise the sugar in a 2-L (2-quart) pot using the method described on page 34. When the sugar has fully caramelised, turn off the heat. Slowly add the cream mixture into the caramelised sugar, being careful of splatter.

● Stir the syrup constantly and gently on medium-high heat, until it reaches 121°C (250°F).

● Pour into the prepared pan, and cover with plastic wrap. Let set overnight at room temperature.

● Unwrap the caramel and place on a cutting board covered with parchment paper. (This will keep the caramel from sticking to the cutting board and also keep any odors from transferring from the board to the candy.) Use a chef's knife or pizza wheel to cut the slab into 1 cm (½-inch) wide strips, and cut each strip into 5-cm (2-inch) long pieces. Wrap each piece individually in cellophane or waxed paper.

VARIATION:

Chocolate Caramels: Omit the vanilla. Add 85 g (3 ounces) chopped dark chocolate to the syrup after the cream has been incorporated into the sugar. Boil to 119°C (247°F).

20 x 20-cm (8 x 8-inch) baking pan

Plastic wrap

1-L (1-quart) saucepan

2-L (2-quart) saucepan

Heatproof silicone spatula

Candy thermometer

Cutting board

Parchment paper

Chef's knife or pizza wheel

Cellophane squares or waxed paper

2 tablespoons corn syrup

4 tablespoons butter, cut into cubes

1 teaspoon kosher salt

240 ml (1 cup) cream

1 vanilla bean, scraped, seeds and pods reserved

400 g (2 cups) sugar

Pumpkin Caramels

MAKES 64 pieces

This is a pumpkin pie transformed into candy – hold the crust! If you can't find golden syrup at your grocery store, you can use molasses instead.

METHOD

● Line an 20 x 20-cm (8 x 8-inch) pan with plastic wrap.

● Mix together the corn syrup, golden syrup, cinnamon, ginger and allspice into a paste in a 1-L (1-quart) saucepan. Add the butter, kosher salt and cream, and cook over medium heat. Once it comes to a boil, decrease the heat to low to keep it warm.

● Meanwhile, caramelise the sugar in a 2-L (2-quart) saucepan using the method described on page 34. When the sugar has fully caramelised, turn off the heat. Slowly add the cream mixture into the sugar, being careful of splatter. Return heat to medium high, and stir until smooth. Add the pumpkin to the syrup, and stir the syrup constantly and gently until it reaches 120°C (248°F).

● Pour into the prepared pan, and cover with plastic wrap. Let set overnight at room temperature.

● Unwrap the caramel and place it on a cutting board covered with parchment paper. (This will keep the caramel from sticking to the cutting board and also keep any odours from transferring from the board to the candy.) Use a chef's knife or pizza wheel to cut the slab into 1-cm (½-inch) wide strips, and cut each strip into 5-cm (2-inch) long pieces. Individually wrap in cellophane or waxed paper.

20 x 20-cm (8 x 8-inch) baking pan

Plastic wrap

1-L (1-quart) saucepan

2-L (2-quart) saucepan

Heatproof silicone spatula

Candy thermometer

Cutting board

Parchment paper

Chef's knife or pizza wheel

Cellophane squares or waxed paper

1   tablespoon corn syrup

1   tablespoon golden syrup or molasses

½ teaspoon cinnamon

¼ teaspoon ginger

⅛ teaspoon allspice

1   tablespoon butter

1¼ teaspoons kosher salt

360 ml (1½ cups) cream

400 g (2 cups) sugar

120 ml (½ cup) pureed pumpkin, canned or fresh

Saltwater Taffy

MAKES ABOUT 900 g *(2 pounds)*

This taffy may seem like a boiled sweet when you first pop it in your mouth, but it will quickly soften and become unabashedly chewy.

METHOD

● Place the silicone mats on the counter.

● Combine the sugar and cornflour in a 3-L (3-quart) saucepan. Add the corn syrup, water, butter and salt, and stir to combine with a heatproof spatula. Wash down any crystals on the side of the pan with a moistened pastry brush. Bring the syrup to a boil over medium heat, stirring gently only until the sugar dissolves.

● Without stirring, cook the syrup to 125.5°C (258°F). Remove from the heat, and stir in the bicarbonate of soda.

● Pour equal amounts of the syrup onto each silicone mat. Pour a few drops of flavouring and colouring in the centre of each slab, then let the taffy sit until it's cool enough to handle.

● With gloved hands, grab the taffy edges and pull into a long strand, fold the strand back together and repeat until the taffy is glossy and firm enough to hold its shape when placed down, about 5 to 10 minutes. Roll taffy into a 1-cm (½-inch)-thick rope and cut into 2.5-cm (1-inch) lengths. Repeat with all slabs. Wrap each piece in a 7.5 x 10-cm (3 x 4-inch) piece of waxed paper.

Tip: *If you make more than one colour of taffy from the same batch, try pulling two different coloured strands together while twisting to make striped taffy.*

Silicone non-stick mats (1 for each flavour or colour of taffy you are making)

3-L (3-quart) saucepan

Heatproof silicone spatula

Pastry brush

Candy thermometer

Food-safe gloves

Chef's knife

Waxed paper

400 g (2 cups) sugar

2 tablespoons cornflour

240 ml (1 cup) light corn syrup

180 ml (¾ cup) water

2 tablespoons butter

¼ teaspoon salt

⅛ teaspoon bicarbonate of soda

Flavouring extract (such as lime, lemon or cherry)

Food colouring, assorted colours

Pecan Pie Taffy

MAKES ABOUT 550 g *(1¹/₄ pounds)*

If you've never made taffy, I can't imagine a better recipe with which to start. You'll marvel at how a dark brown puddle of cooked sugar transforms into a shiny golden rope in your hands. And your reward will taste just like pecan pie!

23 x 33-cm (9 x 13-inch) baking pan

3-L (3-quart) saucepan

Heatproof silicone spatula

Candy thermometer

Food-safe gloves (optional)

Chef's knife

Waxed paper

Oil for the pan

100 g (½ cup) sugar

50 g (⅓ cup) packed dark brown sugar

240 ml (1 cup) light molasses

120 ml (½ cup) water

60 ml (¼ cup) bourbon (optional)

2 tablespoons butter

1/16 teaspoon bicarbonate of soda

⅛ teaspoon kosher salt

1 teaspoon vanilla extract (page 130)

60 g (⅔ cup) pecans, roasted and chopped (page 134)

METHOD

● Coat a 23 x 33-cm (9 x 13-inch) baking pan with oil.

● Bring the sugars, molasses, water and bourbon, if using, to a boil in a 3-L (3-quart) saucepan over medium heat, stirring occasionally with a heatproof spatula.

● Cook to 121°C (250°F), stirring constantly and gently to prevent scorching.

● Remove from the heat. Add the butter, bicarbonate of soda, salt and vanilla, stirring just to incorporate thoroughly.

● Pour into the baking pan and sprinkle on the pecans. Let cool until it is just warm, about 30 minutes.

● With gloved or buttered hands, gather the taffy from the edges and pull until it is lightly colored and firm enough to hold its shape. Roll the taffy into a thin rope and cut it into 2.5-cm (1-inch) lengths. Wrap in waxed paper.

Jelly Candies

MAKES ABOUT 64 pieces

Have fun experimenting with colors to match the flavours of these delightfully chewy jellies.

METHOD

● Line an 20 x 20-cm (8 x 8-inch) baking pan with plastic wrap, and coat with oil.

● Combine the sugar and gelatin in a 5-L (5-quart) pan. Add water and bring to a boil over medium heat, stirring occasionally with a heatproof spatula. Slowly pour in the corn syrup, and return to a gentle boil. Stir the syrup constantly until it reaches 109°C (228°F).

● Remove from the heat, and thoroughly stir in the colouring, flavouring and citric acid. Pour the syrup into the prepared pan. Let cool to room temperature.

● Cover with an oiled piece of plastic wrap and place in the freezer until firm, 1 to 2 hours. Unmould and unwrap the slab onto oiled parchment paper on a cutting board. With a chef's knife, cut jellies into 2.5-cm (1-inch) squares, and toss in sugar to coat. Store in an airtight container.

→ YOU WILL NEED

20 x 20-cm (8 x 8-inch) baking pan

Plastic wrap

5-quart pan

Heatproof silicone spatula

Candy thermometer

Parchment paper

Cutting board

Chef's knife

Oil for the pan

300 g (1½ cups) sugar

4 tablespoons (4 envelopes) unflavoured gelatin

480 ml (2 cups) water

300 ml (1¼ cups) corn syrup

¼ teaspoon liquid food colouring

1 teaspoon flavouring, such as cherry, cinnamon or mint

¼ teaspoon citric acid

Sugar, for coating

Applesauce Jellies

MAKES ABOUT 900 g (2 pounds)

As these jellies cook, the sugar caramelises just enough to make them reminiscent of the autumnal thrill of caramel apples.

METHOD

● Line an 20 x 20-cm (8 x 8-inch) baking pan with plastic wrap and coat evenly with oil.

● Combine sour cream and 1¼ cups of the applesauce in a small bowl. Sprinkle the gelatin on top, and stir until smooth.

● Boil the remaining 300 ml (1 cup) of applesauce and the sugar over medium heat in a 3-L (3-quart) saucepan, stirring occasionally with a heatproof spatula until the sugar dissolves. Add the gelatin mixture in several additions, stirring to dissolve between each. Stir the boiling mixture constantly and gently until it reaches 106.5°C (224°F), about 25 minutes.

● Remove from the heat, and let sit 5 minutes. Stir in the walnuts, if using, vanilla and salt, and pour into the prepared baking pan. Let cool until room temperature, and then refrigerate overnight.

● Cut into 2.5-cm (1-inch) squares with a chef's knife. Roll in the cornflour or powdered sugar. Store in an airtight container.

VARIATION:

Cinnamon Applesauce Jellies: Add 1½ teaspoons cinnamon to the gelatin mixture.

YOU WILL NEED

20 x 20-cm (8 x 8-inch) baking pan

Plastic wrap

Small bowl

3-L (3-quart) saucepan

Heatproof silicone spatula

Candy thermometer

Chef's knife

Oil for the pan

2   tablespoons sour cream

540 ml (2¼ cups) apple-sauce, divided

3   tablespoons (3 envelopes) unflavoured gelatin

550 g (2¾ cups) sugar

110 g (⅔ cup) walnuts, coarsely chopped (optional)

1¼ teaspoons vanilla extract (page 130)

Pinch salt

500 g (2 cups) cornflour or powdered sugar for coating

Fruit Jam Jellies

MAKES 64 pieces

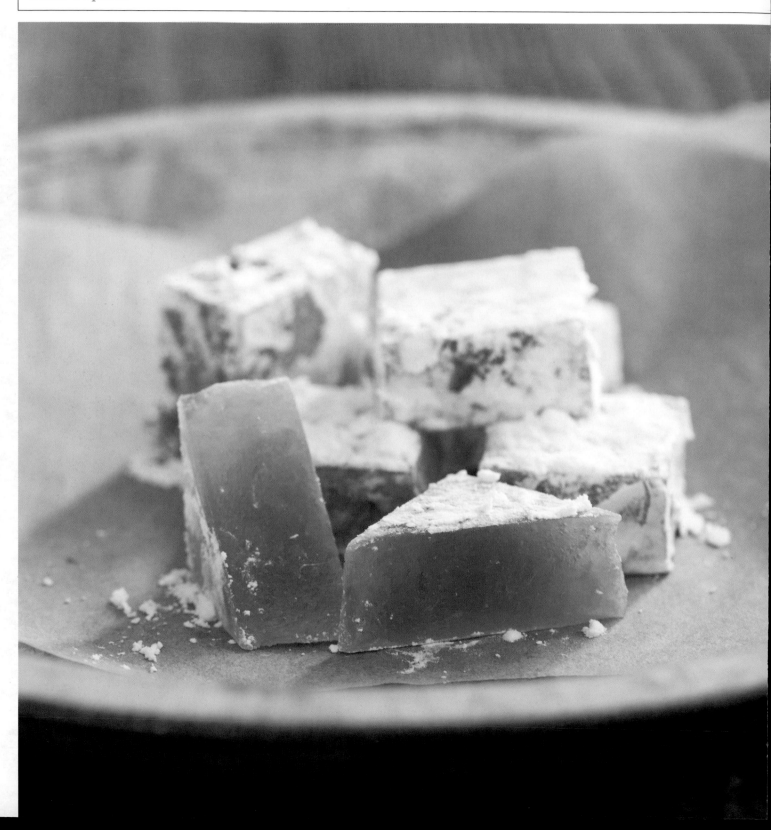

Any flavour of jam you happen to have in your pantry will work to make these simple, delicious candies.

METHOD

● Oil an 20 x 20-cm (8 x 8-inch) baking pan.

● Combine the jam, water, sugar, gelatin and citric acid in a 3-L (3-quart) saucepan. Stir constantly and slowly over medium-high heat with a heatproof spatula until the syrup reaches 104°C (220°F). Pour into the prepared pan, and skim off any foam with a spoon. Let cool to room temperature, and then refrigerate until firm, about 3 hours.

● Combine the powdered sugar and cornflour in a bowl. Unmould the jelly onto a cutting board lined with parchment paper. Cut into 2.5-cm (1-inch) squares and roll in the powdered sugar and cornflour mixture. Store in an airtight container.

20 x 20-cm (8 x 8-inch) baking pan

3-L (3-quart) saucepan

Heatproof silicone spatula

Candy thermometer

Spoon

Bowl

Cutting board

Parchment paper

Oil for the pan

360 ml (1½ cups) jam

180 ml (¾ cup) water

150 g (¾ cup) sugar

3 tablespoons (3 envelopes) unflavoured gelatin

¼ teaspoon citric acid

65 g (⅓ cup) powdered sugar

75 g (⅓ cup) cornflour

Blueberry Coconut Nougat

MAKES ABOUT 128 pieces

Nougat may seem intimidating, but it's really just sugar syrup that's whipped into egg whites, like a thick meringue. The key is to have everything ready when you start because ingredients are added at crucial times. Also, keep in mind that the nougat will need to set overnight.

→ YOU WILL NEED

METHOD

● Line a baking tray with a silicone mat.

● Place the egg whites in the mixing bowl of a 5-L (5-quart) stand mixer.

● Boil the water, sugar, corn syrup, honey and kosher salt in a 2-L (2-quart) saucepan on medium-high heat to 121°C (250°F) without stirring.

● Immediately whisk the egg whites until foamy and add the powdered sugar. Whisk until soft peaks form.

● When the sugar syrup reaches 131°C (268°F), remove from the heat, and slowly pour the syrup down the inside edge of the bowl of whisked egg whites, while whisking by hand to incorporate. Place the bowl in the mixer with the whisk attachment. Mix on the highest speed for 5 minutes. Decrease to low and add the melted cocoa butter down the side of the bowl. Increase mixing speed to high, and mix to incorporate, about 30 seconds. Turn off the mixer and add the coconut. Mix on low speed until incorporated, about 30 seconds.

● Use a rubber spatula to scoop and spread the warm nougat into a 1-cm (½-inch) thick layer on the silicone mat that's on the baking tray.

YOU WILL NEED

Baking tray

2 silicone mats

5-L (5-quart) stand mixer with whisk attachment

2-L (2-quart) saucepan

Candy thermometer

Whisk

Rubber spatula

Plastic wrap

Offset spatula

Cutting board

Parchment paper

Ruler or straightedge

Pizza wheel

Dipping forks

2 egg whites

60 ml (¼ cup) water

300 g (1½ cups) sugar

120 ml (½ cup) corn syrup

120 ml (½ cup) honey

Pinch kosher salt

2½ teaspoons powdered sugar

25 g (1 ounce) cocoa butter, melted

75 g (¾ cup) finely shredded dried coconut, unsweetened

900 g (2 pounds) dark chocolate, tempered (page 20) or coating chocolate, melted

85 g (½ cup) dried blueberries

The nougat will be about 20 x 40 cm (8 x 16 inches). Immediately cover with the second silicone mat. When cool, wrap the entire assemblage (baking tray, silicone mat, nougat and second silicone mat) in plastic wrap. Let set overnight at room temperature.

● Unwrap the assemblage, and peel the top silicone mat off the nougat. Use the offset spatula to spread tempered chocolate in a thin layer on the top of the nougat slab. Let set, and flip the slab, chocolate side down, onto a cutting board covered with parchment paper. Peel off the second silicone mat, and spread a thin layer of tempered chocolate on the second side of the nougat. Keep the leftover chocolate at temperature for dipping. Use the ruler or straightedge and pizza wheel to cut the nougat into 2.5-cm (1-inch) squares. Dip the squares in the reserved tempered chocolate according to the instructions on page 27. Depending on the size of the dried blueberries, place 1 to 3 blueberries on top of each piece before the chocolate sets. Store in an airtight container.

Caramel Pinwheels

MAKES ABOUT 128 pieces

These eye-catching sweets let you mix flavours of caramels in a unique way. Once you've got the technique down, experiment with different flavour combinations.

YOU WILL NEED

Plastic wrap

Cutting board

Parchment paper

Pizza wheel

Chef's knife

Cellophane squares

20 x 20-cm (8 x 8-inch) slab of chocolate caramel (page 69)

20 x 20-cm (8 x 8-inch) slab of vanilla (or pumpkin) caramel (page 68 or 70)

METHOD

● Place the slab of chocolate caramel on a piece of plastic wrap. Use the palm of your hand to push down and outwards on the caramel so that it thins and elongates into a slab that's about 20 x 40 cm (8 x 16 inches). Repeat with the other slab of caramel on another piece of plastic wrap.

● Carefully place one slab of caramel atop the other on a cutting board covered with parchment paper. (This will keep the caramel from sticking to the cutting board and also keep any odours from transferring from the board to the candy.) Use a pizza wheel to cut this double slab of caramel in half lengthways into two 10-cm (4-inch)-wide slabs. Starting at one of the long edges of a slab, roll the caramel tightly into a log shape. Repeat with the remaining slab.

● Use a chef's knife to cut each log into two pieces. With your fingers extended, roll each log, one at a time, in the palms of your hands until it elongates and becomes thinner, about 2.5 cm (1 inch) in diameter. Cut each log into 2.5-cm (1-inch) pieces, and wrap in cellophane.

Orange Walnut Chocolate Nougat

*MAKES **128** pieces*

In some ways, this nougat is like a tricked-out brownie – chocolatey, chewy, nutty and intriguingly spiked with orange.

METHOD

● Line a baking tray with one silicone mat.

● Place the egg whites in the mixing bowl of a 5-L (5-quart) stand mixer.

● Boil the water, sugar, corn syrup, honey and kosher salt in a 2-L (2-quart) saucepan on medium-high heat to 121°C (250°F) without stirring.

● Immediately whisk the egg whites until foamy and add the powdered sugar. Whisk until soft peaks form.

● When the sugar syrup reaches 132°C (270°F), remove from the heat, and slowly pour the syrup down the inside edge of the bowl of whisked egg whites, while whisking by hand to incorporate. Place the bowl in the mixer with the whisk attachment. Mix on the highest speed for 5 minutes. Decrease to low and add the melted unsweetened chocolate down the side of the bowl. Increase to high speed and mix to incorporate, about 30 seconds. Turn off the mixer and add the walnuts. Mix on low speed until incorporated, about 30 seconds.

● Use a rubber spatula to scoop and spread the warm nougat into a 1-cm (½-inch) thick layer on the silicone mat that's on the baking tray. The nougat will be about 20 x 40 cm (8 x 16 inches). Immediately cover with the second silicone mat. When cool, wrap the entire assemblage (baking tray, silicone mat, nougat and second silicone mat) in plastic wrap. Let set overnight at room temperature.

● Unwrap the assemblage, and peel the top silicone mat off the nougat. Use the offset spatula to spread tempered chocolate in a thin layer on the top of the nougat slab. Let set, and flip the slab, chocolate side down, onto a cutting board covered with parchment paper. Peel off the second silicone mat, and spread a thin layer of tempered chocolate on the second side of the nougat. Keep the leftover chocolate at temperature for dipping. Use the ruler or straightedge and pizza wheel to cut the nougat into 2.5-cm (1-inch) squares. Dip according to the instructions on page 27. Press a piece of crystallised orange peel on top of each piece before the chocolate sets for garnish. Store in an airtight container.

Baking tray

2 silicone mats

5-L (5-quart) stand mixer with whisk attachment

2-L (2-quart) saucepan

Candy thermometer

Whisk

Rubber spatula

Plastic wrap

Offset spatula

Cutting board

Parchment paper

Ruler or straightedge

Pizza wheel

Dipping forks

2 egg whites

60 ml (¼ cup) water

300 g (1½ cups) sugar

120 ml (½ cup) corn syrup

120 ml (½ cup) honey

Pinch kosher salt

2½ teaspoons powdered sugar

55 g (2 ounces) unsweetened chocolate, melted

100 g (1 cup) walnuts, roasted and finely chopped (page 134)

900 g (2 pounds) tempered dark chocolate (page 20) or melting chocolate

64 pieces of crystallised orange peel (page 132), ½ inch each

Peach Turkish Delights

MAKES *64 pieces*

The luscious texture of Turkish delights is the perfect platform for a peach candy. The roasted almonds complement the flavour and diffuse the sweetness.

20 x 20-cm (8 x 8-inch) baking pan

Plastic wrap

1-L (1-quart) saucepan

Candy thermometer

Whisk

3-L (3-quart) saucepan

Chef's knife

Oil for the pan

480 ml (2 cups) water, divided

400 g (2 cups) sugar

1   teaspoon lemon juice

110 g (½ cup) cornflour

½ teaspoon cream of tartar

1   teaspoon peach flavouring

1   drop orange colouring

1   drop yellow colouring

55 g (½ cup) almonds, roasted and coarsely chopped (page 134)

100 g (½ cup) powdered sugar

METHOD

● Line an 20 x 20-cm (8 x 8-inch) pan with plastic wrap and coat with oil.

● Combine 120 ml (½ cup) of the water, the sugar and the lemon juice in a 1-L (1-quart) saucepan, and boil to 126.5°C (260°F) over medium-high heat without stirring. Remove from the heat.

● Whisk together the cornflour, cream of tartar and 360 ml (1½ cups) of the water in a 3-quart saucepan. Bring to a boil over medium heat, and whisk for 5 minutes. It will be very thick.

● Add half of the sugar syrup to the cornflour mixture, and whisk to incorporate. Add the remaining half, and whisk to incorporate. Continue whisking on medium-low heat until smooth and clear, about 20 to 25 minutes.

● Remove from the heat, and whisk in peach flavouring, colourings and almonds. Pour into the prepared pan, and let cool to room temperature. Cover pan in plastic wrap, and let set overnight at room temperature.

● Cut into 2.5-cm (1-inch) pieces, and roll in powdered sugar to coat. Store in an airtight container.

Sugarplums

MAKES ABOUT 225 g (¹/₂ *pound*)

If you've ever had visions of sugarplums dancing in your head (and who hasn't?), you'll enjoy making these delectable holiday treats. They come together in a snap, and their flavour continues to develop over time.

YOU WILL NEED

3 bowls

Food processor

100 g (½ cup) sugar

¼ teaspoon allspice

¼ teaspoon cardamom

¼ teaspoon cinnamon

25 g (¼ cup) pistachios, roasted (page 134)

50 g (½ cup) almonds, roasted (page 134)

175 g (1 cup) dried plums (not prunes)

175 g (1 cup) dates

85 g (½ cup) dried apricots

2 tablespoons honey

½ teaspoon rosewater

METHOD

● In a medium bowl, combine the sugar, allspice, cardamom and cinnamon.

● Use a food processor to finely chop the pistachios and almonds. Transfer the chopped nuts to a bowl, and reserve.

● In the food processor, chop the plums, dates, apricots and honey until they just begin to clump. Add the reserved nuts and the rosewater, and process until the mixture forms a ball.

● Transfer the mixture to a clean bowl, and roll into 2.5-cm (1-inch) diameter balls. Roll each ball in the sugar and spice mixture to cover completely, and store in the refrigerator in an airtight container.

Tip: *Dried plums look like flattened halves of plums. They are more tart and flavourful than prunes. If dried plums are unavailable, use dried figs instead.*

Silky Candy

Chocolate Fudge

MAKES ONE 20 x 20-cm (8 x 8-inch) slab of fudge

Luscious, silken and an all-time champ in the candy world, this classic fudge will please every sweet tooth.

METHOD

● Oil an 20 x 20-cm (8 x 8-inch) baking pan.

● Bring the sugar, cream, milk, corn syrup and salt to a boil over medium heat in a 3-L (3-quart) saucepan, stirring occasionally with a heatproof spatula. Add the chocolate, and boil to 114.5°C (238°F), stirring frequently. Remove from the heat, and stir in the vanilla extract.

● Pour the syrup in a thin layer in a 23 x 33-cm (9 x 13-inch) baking pan. Let cool to 43°C (110°F) undisturbed, about 20 minutes. Scrape the syrup into the bowl of a stand mixer.

● Mix on medium speed with a paddle attachment until the fudge thickens and begins to hold its shape, about 7 minutes. Scrape into the prepared 20 x 20-cm (8 x 8-inch) pan, and spread evenly with an offset spatula. Let set for at least 2 hours at room temperature. Cut into pieces of desired size, and store in an airtight container.

VARIATION:

Chocolate Ginger Fudge: Add 50 g (⅓ cup) finely chopped crystallised ginger (page 136) after 2 minutes of mixing. Sprinkle with an additional 35 g (¼ cup) of finely chopped crystallised ginger once the fudge has been spread in the 20 x 20-cm (8 x 8-inch) pan.

20 x 20-cm (8 x 8-inch) baking pan

3-L (3-quart) saucepan

Heatproof silicone spatula

Candy thermometer

23 x 33-cm (9 x 13-inch) baking pan

5-L (5-quart) stand mixer

Offset spatula

Chef's knife

Oil for the pan

400 g (2 cups) sugar

120 ml (½ cup) cream

60 ml (¼ cup) milk

60 ml (¼ cup) corn syrup

¾ teaspoon kosher salt

115 g (4 ounces) unsweetened chocolate, finely chopped

1½ teaspoons vanilla extract (page 130)

Vanilla Cheesecake Fudge

MAKES ONE 20-cm (8-inch) diameter circular slab

Creamy, tangy and full of vanilla, this unique fudge will satisfy any
and all cheesecake cravings. Using a round cake pan to mould the fudge
will add to the presentation.

METHOD

● Oil an 20-cm (8-inch) round cake pan.

● Bring the sugar, corn syrup, milk and vanilla seeds to a boil in a 3-L
(3-quart) saucepan over medium heat, stirring occasionally with a
heatproof spatula. Boil to 121°C (250°F), stirring frequently. The syrup
will become a light brown colour.

● Pour the mixture into a 23 x 33-cm (9 x 13-inch) baking pan, and let
cool to 49°C (120°F), about 20 minutes.

● Scrape the syrup into the bowl of a stand mixer, and add the cream
cheese and salt. Mix on medium speed with the paddle attachment for
15 seconds. Scrape down the sides of the mixing bowl, and then mix
on high speed until the mixture thickens slightly and begins to hold its
shape, about 10 minutes.

● Pour into the prepared cake pan, and sprinkle with the dried fruit.
Let cool to room temperature. Refrigerate overnight.

● Unmould from the pan and cut in wedge-shaped cake slices. Store in
an airtight container in the refrigerator.

Tip: *For a gift, separate slices with pieces of waxed paper to mimic a*
traditional cheesecake presentation.

20-cm (8-inch) round
cake pan

3-L (3-quart) saucepan

Heatproof silicone spatula

Candy thermometer

23 x 33-cm (9 x 13-inch)
baking pan

5-L (5-quart) stand mixer

Oil for the pan

800 g (4 cups) sugar

120 ml (½ cup) corn syrup

175 g (6 ounces) milk

1   vanilla bean, scraped,
seeds only

115 g (4 ounces)
cream cheese

¼ teaspoon kosher salt

55 g (⅓ cup) dried fruit,
such as cherries or
blueberries

Chocolate Chip Cookie Dough Fudge

MAKES ONE 20 x 20-cm (8 x 8-inch) slab

Penuche is a classic brown sugar fudge with ingredients almost identical to those of chocolate chip cookies. This recipe riff bridges the gap between sweet and cookie with delicious results.

METHOD

● Oil an 20 x 20 cm (8 x 8-inch) baking pan.

● Bring the sugar, dark brown sugar, cream, milk, corn syrup and salt to a boil over medium heat in a 3-L (3-quart) saucepan, stirring occasionally with a heatproof spatula. Boil to 116.5°C (242°F), stirring frequently. Remove from the heat and stir in the butter, vanilla and flour. Pour the syrup into a 23 x 33-cm (9 x 13-inch) baking pan in a thin layer. Let cool to 43°C (110°F) undisturbed at room temperature, about 20 minutes. Scrape the syrup into the bowl of a stand mixer.

● Mix on medium speed with a paddle attachment until the fudge thickens and begins to hold its shape, 3 to 5 minutes. Scrape into the prepared 20 x 20-cm (8 x 8-inch) baking pan, and spread evenly with an offset spatula. Sprinkle the chocolate chips on top, then lightly press them into the fudge. Let cool and set, at least 2 hours. Chill in the fridge for about 30 minutes if the chocolate chips are still soft. Cut into pieces of desired size, and store in an airtight container.

20 x 20-cm (8 x 8-inch) baking pan

3-L (3-quart) saucepan

Heatproof silicone spatula

Candy thermometer

23 x 33-cm (9 x 13-inch) baking pan

5-L (5-quart) stand mixer

Offset spatula

Chef's knife

Oil for the pan

550 g (1¾ cups) sugar

110 g (¾ cup) dark brown sugar

120 ml (½ cup) cream

60 ml (¼ cup) milk

1 tablespoon corn syrup

¾ teaspoon kosher salt

2 tablespoons butter

1 teaspoon vanilla extract (page 130)

55 g (½ cup) flour

50 g (⅓ cup) chocolate chips

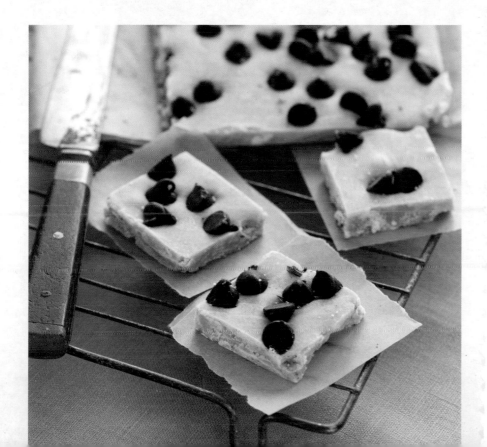

Mixed-Nut Dark Chocolate Truffles

MAKES ABOUT 35 truffles

In a perfect world, these intense shots of pure chocolate pleasure
would always be waiting in the refrigerator: cool and creamy with just
the right accent of nutty flavour.

→ YOU WILL NEED

METHOD

● Use a food processor to finely chop the roughly chopped chocolate.

● Bring the corn syrup, salt and cream to a boil over medium-high heat
in a 1-L (1-quart) saucepan without stirring.

● Pour the cream mixture over the chocolate, and process for
30 seconds. Scrape down the sides of the food processor bowl with
a heatproof spatula. Process for 30 seconds more, or until completely
smooth. Pour the mixture into a stainless steel bowl, and cover directly
with plastic wrap. Refrigerate until firm, about 3 hours.

● Process the almonds, pecans, walnuts and sea salt in the clean bowl
of the food processor until finely ground, about 20 seconds. Pour the
mixture into a clean stainless steel bowl. Use a miniature ice cream
scoop or melon baller to form 2.5-cm (1-inch)-diameter truffles, roll
each lightly by hand and then roll each truffle in the nut mixture until
fully coated. Store in an airtight container in the refrigerator.

YOU WILL NEED

Food processor

1-L (1-quart) saucepan

Heatproof silicone spatula

2 stainless steel bowls

Plastic wrap

Miniature ice cream scoop
or melon baller

Food-safe gloves

250 g (9 ounces) dark
chocolate, chopped

1　tablespoon corn syrup

Pinch kosher salt

240 ml (1 cup) cream

30 g (⅓ cup) roasted
almonds (page 134)

30 g (⅓ cup) roasted
pecans

30 g (⅓ cup) roasted
walnuts

1½ teaspoons sea salt

Pear Hazelnut Truffles

MAKES 64 truffles

Pears and hazelnuts are treasures of the Pacific Northwest – the addition of chocolate makes them out of this world.

METHOD

● Line an 20 x 20-cm (8 x 8-inch) baking pan with plastic wrap.

● Use a food processor to finely chop the coarsely chopped white and milk chocolates.

● Bring the cream and salt to a boil over medium-high heat in a 1-L (1-quart) saucepan. Add the pear liqueur, and immediately pour the cream mixture over the chopped chocolate. Process for 30 seconds. Scrape down the sides of the food processor bowl with a heatproof spatula. Process for 1 minute more, or until completely smooth.

● Pour the mixture into the prepared pan, and smooth the top with an offset spatula. Cover with plastic wrap and let set overnight in a cool room.

● Remove the wrapped slab from the baking pan, and place it on a cutting board. Use the offset spatula to spread a thin layer of the tempered chocolate on the slab. Let set, and then flip over onto a piece of parchment paper, and spread a thin layer of chocolate on the second side.

● Score the slab into 2.5-cm (1-inch)-square pieces with a ruler or straightedge and a pizza wheel before the chocolate sets. Cut a row at a time into squares, and dip according to the instructions on page 27. Garnish with a triangle of dried pear on one corner and a half hazelnut on the diagonal corner.

dip according to the instructions on page 27

20 x 20-cm (8 x 8-inch) baking pan

Plastic wrap

Food processor

1-L (1-quart) saucepan

Heatproof silicone spatula

Offset spatula

Cutting board

Parchment paper

Ruler or straightedge

Pizza wheel

Chef's knife

Dipping forks

280 g (10 ounces) white chocolate, coarsely chopped

55 g (2 ounces) milk chocolate, coarsely chopped

115 g (4 ounces) cream

Pinch kosher salt

4 teaspoons pear liqueur

900 g (2 pounds) milk chocolate, tempered (page 20)

64 dried pear pieces, cut into triangles with two 1-cm (½-inch) sides

32 hazelnuts, roasted, skinned and cut in half (page 134)

Piña Colada Truffles

MAKES 64 truffles

Complete with a glacé cherry, bits of pineapple and coconut, these truffles will practically whisk you away to a sandy beach with your first bite.

METHOD

● Line an 20 x 20-cm (8 x-8-inch) baking pan with plastic wrap.

● Use a food processor to finely chop the coarsely chopped white chocolate. Bring the cream, coconut milk and salt to a boil over medium-high heat in a 1-L (1-quart) saucepan. Add the rum, and immediately pour the cream mixture over the chocolate. Process for 30 seconds. Scrape down the sides of the food processor bowl with a heatproof spatula. Process for 1 minute more, or until completely smooth. Add the crystallised pineapple, and process for 15 seconds more. Pour the mixture into the prepared pan and smooth the top with an offset spatula. Cover with plastic wrap and let set overnight in a cool room.

● Remove the wrapped slab from the baking pan, and place it on a cutting board. Use an offset spatula to spread a thin layer of the tempered white chocolate on the slab. Let set, and then flip over onto a piece of parchment paper, and spread a thin layer of white chocolate on the second side.

● Score the slab into 2.5-cm (1-inch)-square pieces with a ruler or straightedge and a pizza wheel before the chocolate sets. Cut a row at a time into squares, and dip according to the instructions on page 27. Garnish with coconut and a glacé cherry sliver.

YOU WILL NEED

20 x 20-cm (8 x 8-inch) baking pan

Plastic wrap

Food processor

1-L (1-quart) saucepan

Heatproof silicone spatula

Offset spatula

Cutting board

Parchment paper

Ruler or straightedge

Pizza wheel

Chef's knife

Dipping forks

350 g (12 ounces) white chocolate, coarsely chopped

60 ml (2 ounces) cream

30 ml (1 ounce) coconut milk

Pinch kosher salt

1 tablespoon dark rum

¼ cup finely chopped crystallised pineapple, about 1 ring

900 g (2 pounds) white chocolate, tempered (page 20)

120 ml (½ cup) finely shredded dried coconut, unsweetened

8 glacé cherries, each cut into 8 slices

Divinity Sundaes

MAKES 36 pieces

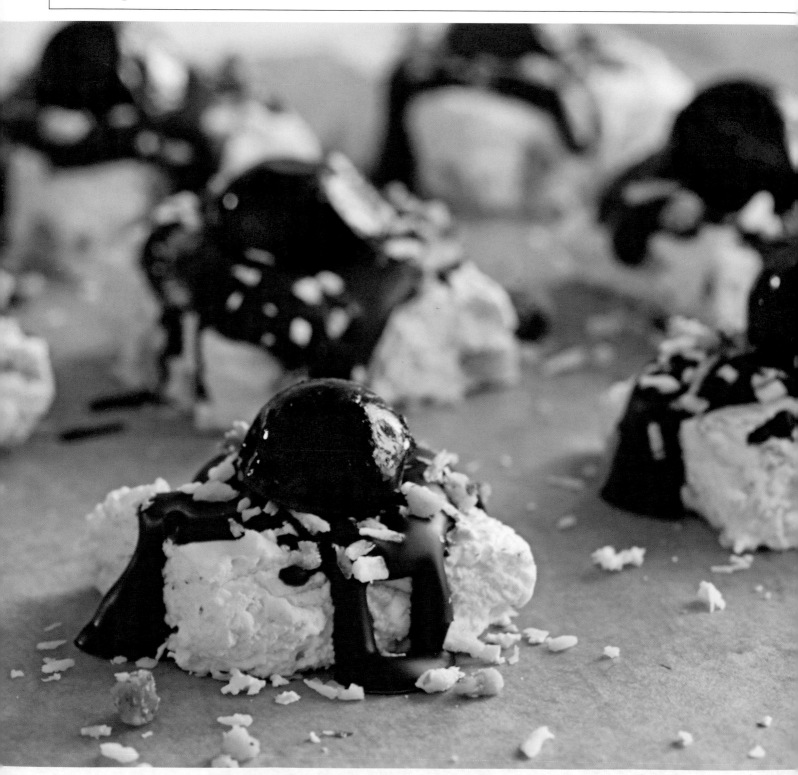

Divinity is a thick meringue-like candy that is less dense and less chewy than nougat and commonly associated with the American South. Its name comes from its divinely light and airy texture, and decorating this confection like a miniature ice cream sundae just completes the delicious effect.

METHOD

● Line an 20 x 20-cm (8 x 8-inch) baking pan with parchment paper, and oil the parchment.

● Place the egg whites and 2 tablespoons of the sugar in the bowl of a stand mixer.

● Bring the water, 400 g (2 cups) sugar and corn syrup to a boil in a 2-L (2-quart) saucepan over medium-high heat, stirring occasionally with a heatproof spatula until the sugar is dissolved. When the syrup reaches 115.5°C (240°F), whip the egg whites mixture on high speed to form very stiff peaks. Then whip the egg whites on low until the syrup reaches 122°C (252°F).

Tip: *If the egg whites don't stay in motion once they are whipped, they'll separate (water will collect underneath), and if they are kept on high speed, they'll also separate. It should only take a couple minutes for the syrup to reach 122°C (252°F).*

● Pour the syrup down the side of the mixer bowl containing the whipped egg whites, and mix on high. While mixing, slowly pour the vanilla extract down the side of the bowl, and continue mixing until the divinity becomes slightly dull and thick enough to completely hold its shape, about 10 minutes. Turn the mixer to low speed, and add the walnuts and kosher salt. Scrape the divinity into the prepared pan, and spread evenly with an offset spatula. Let cool at room temperature.

● Unmould the slab of divinity, and use a ruler or straightedge to cut the slab into roughly 3 x 3 cm (1¼ x 1¼-inch) squares. Drizzle tempered dark chocolate on top of each square so that a little runs over each edge. Sprinkle on the toppings, and place a glacé cherry half on top of each square.

20 x 20-cm (8 x 8-inch) baking pan

Parchment paper

5-L (5-quart) stand mixer

2-L (2-quart) saucepan

Heatproof silicone spatula

Candy thermometer

Offset spatula

Ruler or straightedge

Chef's knife

Oil for the pan

2 large egg whites

2 tablespoons plus 400 g (2 cups) sugar, divided

120 ml (½ cup) water

120 ml (½ cup) corn syrup

1 teaspoon vanilla extract (page 130)

100 g (1 cup) walnuts, chopped

¼ teaspoon kosher salt

115 g (4 ounces) dark chocolate, tempered (page 20) or coating chocolate, melted

45 g (⅓ cup) toppings, such as sprinkles, finely chopped nuts or coconut

18 glacé cherries, cut in half

Chocolate Caramallows

*MAKES ABOUT **40** pieces*

Chocolate and vanilla are a classic pairing for a reason: Each heightens the flavour of the other, and the addition of salt – perhaps the ultimate flavour enhancer – makes for a confection that's deviously addictive.

→ YOU WILL NEED

Plastic wrap

Chef's knife

40 rectangles of parchment paper, about 15 x 10 cm (6 x 4 inches) each

1 slab of chocolate caramel, 20 x 20 cm (8 x 8 inches) (page 69)

40 vanilla marshmallows (page 116)

Flakey sea salt (optional)

METHOD

● Place the 20 x 20 cm (8 x 8 inch) slab of chocolate caramel on a large piece of plastic wrap. With the palm of your hand, push down and outwards on the caramel so that it thins and elongates. Work with the caramel until it's about 20 x 50 cm (8 x 20 inches).

● Use a chef's knife to cut a 2.5-cm (1-inch)-wide strip of caramel from an 20-cm (8-inch) end of the slab. Place a marshmallow on one end, and roll the strip of caramel around it. Cut the strip where it starts to overlap, and pinch the two ends of the caramel strip together to make the wrapping continuous. Sprinkle with salt, if desired. Wrap in parchment paper. Repeat until you run out of caramel or marshmallows.

Dot Candy

MAKES ABOUT 225 g (½ pound)

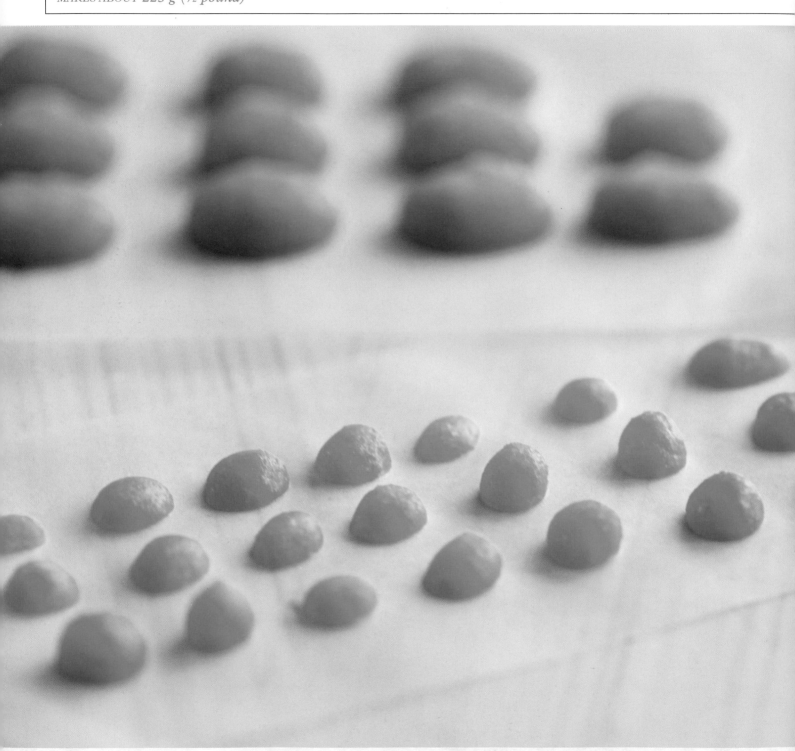

These candies have a compelling crystallised texture and can be created in an array of colours and flavours. A very steady hand is required to make the small dots that we all remember from old-fashioned dot candy, so feel free to make big ones – they're just as fun and delicious.

Parchment paper

1-L (1-quart) saucepan

Pastry brush

Candy thermometer

Stainless steel spoon

200 g (1 cup) sugar

3 tablespoons cream

2 tablespoons water

1 teaspoon butter

5 drops flavouring extract, such as mint, cherry or lemon

3 drops food colouring, such as blue, red or yellow

METHOD

● Line your counter with parchment paper.

● Combine the sugar, cream and water in a 1-L (1-quart) saucepan, and stir gently. Wash down any crystals on the sides of the pan with a moistened pastry brush. Cook syrup to 115.5°C (240°F) over medium heat without stirring.

● Remove from the heat, and with a stainless steel spoon, stir in the butter, flavoring extract and food colouring. Stir until the syrup thickens slightly, about 1 minute, and then drop from the tip of the spoon onto the parchment paper to form the dots. Cut the parchment paper into strips.

Peanut Butter & Maple Pralines

Move over, peanut butter and jelly. Peanut butter and maple syrup are a combination to be reckoned with – as you'll discover when you bite into one of these unique sweets.

YOU WILL NEED

METHOD

● Line a baking tray with parchment paper.

● Boil the maple syrup and corn syrup over medium heat in a 2-L (2-quart) saucepan to 113.5°C (236°F), stirring occasionally with a heatproof spatula. Remove the syrup from the heat, and stir in the peanut butter and salt until they are incorporated. Stir in the peanuts and oats. Quickly drop by spoonfuls onto the parchment paper. If desired, sprinkle flakey sea salt on top. Let cool at room temperature. Store on layers of parchment paper in an airtight container. The pralines will be sticky on the first day, and then they'll crystallise overnight.

Baking tray

Parchment paper

2-L (2-quart) saucepan

Candy thermometer

Heatproof silicone spatula

Large spoon

300 ml (1¼ cups) maple syrup

60 ml (¼ cup) corn syrup

115 g (½ cup) peanut butter

1 teaspoon kosher salt

100 g (1 cup) peanuts, roasted

125 g (1¼ cups) oats

Flakey sea salt, for sprinkling (optional)

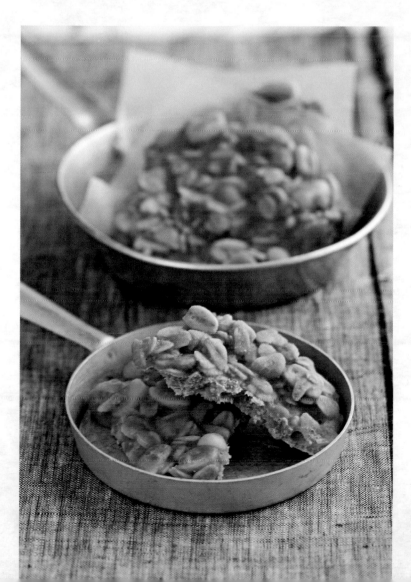

Vanilla Marshmallows

MAKES 96 marshmallows

Perfect with rich hot cocoa or enjoyed simply on their own, homemade marshmallows are tastier, fluffier and fresher than anything you can buy.

METHOD

● Spray a 25 x 38 cm (10 x 15-inch) jellyroll pan liberally with oil.

● Pour 180 ml (¾ cup) cold water into the bowl of a stand mixer, and sprinkle the gelatin on top. Stir with a fork until the gelatin is moistened and free of lumps.

● Bring 240 ml (1 cup) water, sugar, cream of tartar and salt to a boil in a 3-L (3-quart) saucepan over medium-high heat, stirring occasionally with a heatproof spatula until the sugar dissolves. If necessary, wash down the sides of the pan with a wet pastry brush to dissolve any sugar granules. Boil to 121°C (250°F). Remove from the heat, and let cool to 100°C (212°F), about 15 minutes.

● Meanwhile, use a heatproof spatula to break the bloomed gelatin in the mixer bowl into small pieces. When the syrup has cooled to 100°C (212°F), pour it over the gelatin, and stir until the gelatin is melted. Whip with the whisk attachment in the stand mixer for 1 minute on low speed. Increase speed to high, and whip for about 5 minutes, until very fluffy and thick. Add the vanilla extract down the side of the bowl, and whip for 30 seconds more. Pour the mixture into the prepared jellyroll pan, and spread evenly with an offset spatula. Let set overnight.

● Mix the cornflour and powdered sugar in a large bowl. Remove the marsh-mallow slab from the pan and place it on a cutting board. Use a chef's knife and a ruler or straightedge to cut the marshmallows into 3-cm (1¼-inch) squares, tossing with the cornflour mixture to prevent sticking. Shake the marshmallows in a sieve to remove any excess cornflour, and store in an airtight container.

YOU WILL NEED

25 x 38 cm (10 x 15-inch) jellyroll pan

5-L (5-quart) stand mixer with whisk attachment

Fork

3-L (3-quart) saucepan

Heatproof silicone spatula

Pastry brush

Candy thermometer

Offset spatula

Large bowl

Cutting board

Chef's knife

Ruler or straightedge

Sieve

Oil for the pan

180 ml (¾ cup) cold water

3 tablespoons (3 envelopes) unflavoured gelatin

240 ml (1 cup) water

650 g (3¼ cups) sugar

½ teaspoon cream of tartar

⅛ teaspoon kosher salt

¾ teaspoon vanilla extract (page 130)

225 g (1 cup) cornflour

100 g (½ cup) powdered sugar

Strawberry Lemonade Marshmallows

MAKES 192 marshmallows

This pretty two-layer marshmallow will surprise you with its uncanny resemblance to a favourite summer beverage.

METHOD

● Spray two 25 x 38 cm (10 x 15-inch) jellyroll pans liberally with oil.

● For the lemon marshmallow layer, pour 60 ml (¼ cup) cold water and the lemon juice into the bowl of the stand mixer, and sprinkle the gelatin on top. Stir with a fork until the gelatin is moistened and free of lumps.

● Bring 240 ml (1 cup) water, sugar, cream of tartar and salt to a boil in a 3-L (3-quart) saucepan over medium-high heat, stirring occasionally with a heatproof spatula until the sugar dissolves. If necessary, wash down the sides of the pan with a wet pastry brush to dissolve any sugar granules. Boil to 121°C (250°F). Remove from the heat, and let cool to 100°C (212°F), about 15 minutes.

● Meanwhile, use the heatproof spatula to break the bloomed gelatin in the mixer bowl into small pieces. When the syrup has cooled to 100°C (212°F), pour it over the gelatin and stir until the gelatin is melted.

● Whip the mixture with the whisk attachment in the stand mixer for 1 minute on low speed. Increase speed to high, and whip for about 5 minutes, until the mixture is very fluffy and beginning to hold its shape. Add the lemon zest, and whip for 30 seconds more. Pour half of the mixture into each prepared pan, and, working quickly, spread each evenly with an offset spatula. Then make the strawberry marshmallow layer.

● For the strawberry marshmallow layer, place the puréed strawberries in the bowl of the stand mixer, sprinkle the gelatin on top of the strawberries and stir with a fork until the gelatin is moistened and free of lumps.

● Bring 240 ml (1 cup) water, sugar, cream of tartar and salt to a boil in a 3-L (3-quart) saucepan over medium-high heat, stirring occasionally with a heatproof spatula until the sugar dissolves. If necessary, wash down the sides of the pan with a wet pastry brush to dissolve any sugar granules. Boil to 121°C (250°F). Remove from the heat, and let cool to 100°C (212°F).

(continued)

Two 25 x 38 cm (10 x 15-inch) jellyroll pans

5-L 9 (5-quart) stand mixer

Fork

3-L (3-quart) saucepan

Heatproof silicone spatula

Pastry brush

Candy thermometer

Offset spatula

Large bowl

Cutting board

Chef's knife

Ruler or straightedge

Sieve

FOR THE LEMON MARSHMALLOW LAYER:

Oil for the pans

60 ml (¼ cup) cold water

120 ml (½ cup) lemon juice

3 tablespoons (3 envelopes) unflavoured gelatin

240 ml (1 cup) water

650 g (3¼ cups) sugar

½ teaspoon cream of tartar

⅛ teaspoon kosher salt

1 teaspoon lemon zest, finely grated

FOR THE STRAWBERRY MARSHMALLOW LAYER:

180 ml (¾ cup) puréed strawberries (about 350 g/12 ounces strawberries)

3 tablespoons (3 envelopes) unflavoured gelatin

240 ml (1 cup) water

650 g (3¼ cups) sugar

½ teaspoon cream of tartar

⅛ teaspoon kosher salt

500 g (2 cups) cornflour

200 g (1 cup) powdered sugar

● Meanwhile, use a heatproof spatula to break the bloomed gelatin in the mixer bowl into small pieces. When the syrup has cooled to 100°C (212°F), pour it over the gelatin, and stir until the gelatin is melted.

● Place the bowl in the mixer, and whip with the whisk attachment for 1 minute on low speed. Increase the speed to high, and whip for about 5 minutes, until the mixture is very fluffy and beginning to hold its shape. Pour half of the strawberry mixture into each prepared pan on top of the lemon marshmallow layer, and, working quickly, spread each evenly with an offset spatula. Let set overnight.

● Mix the cornflour and powdered sugar in a large bowl. Remove the marshmallow slabs from the pans and place them on a cutting board. Use the chef's knife and the ruler or straightedge to cut the marshmallows into 3 cm (1¼-inch) squares, tossing with the cornflour mixture to prevent sticking. Shake the marshmallows in the sieve to remove any excess cornflour, and store in an airtight container.

Chocolate Stars

MAKES 36 stars

This technique can be used for chocolate moulds of any shape and with any type of chocolate, but only white chocolate can be coloured to impressive effect. The addition of lustre dust, an edible powder that sparkles when it dries, adds shimmery appeal to these treats.

→

YOU WILL NEED

Narrow paintbrush (if using optional lustre dust)

3 star-shaped chocolate moulds with 12 cavities each

Large spoon

Offset spatula

Parchment paper

Edible luster dust (optional)

Dry powder food coloring such as red, white, blue or yellow (optional)

350 g (12 ounces) white chocolate, tempered (page 20), or melting chocolate

METHOD

● Use a narrow paintbrush to apply the luster dust, if using, to each cavity of the moulds.

● Mix food colouring, if using, into the tempered white chocolate. Use a large spoon to fill each cavity to the top with chocolate. Tap the moulds on the counter to release any air bubbles. Remove any excess chocolate by scraping the top of the moulds with an offset spatula. Refrigerate until set, about 20 minutes. Unmould by flipping the moulds upside down on a piece of parchment paper, and tapping on the edge of the mould with the handle of an offset spatula. Store in an airtight container.

Coconut Shells

MAKES 40 shells

With a creamy marshmallow filling and a glossy chocolate shell, these show-stopping chocolates look and taste like coconuts. If you don't have enough moulds to make the full recipe, have an oiled pan ready to pour the extra marshmallow into for free-form snacking.

→ YOU WILL NEED

METHOD

● With a narrow silicone brush, paint three tempered dark chocolate dots in each mould. These will be the "eyes" of the coconut. With a wide silicone brush, paint a 3-mm (⅛-inch)-thick layer of tempered milk chocolate in each mould. Scrape off any uneven tops with an offset spatula. This step can be done in advance.

● In the bowl of a stand mixer, sprinkle the gelatin on top of 180 ml (¾ cup) cold water, and stir with a fork until the gelatin is moistened and free of lumps.

● Bring 240 ml (1 cup) water, sugar, cream of tartar and salt to a boil in a 3-L (3-quart) saucepan over medium-high heat, stirring occasionally with a heatproof spatula until the sugar dissolves. If sugar crystals cling to the sides of the pan, dissolve them away with a wet pastry brush. Boil to 121°C (250°F). Remove the syrup from the heat, and let cool to 100°C (212°F), about 15 minutes.

● Meanwhile, use the heatproof spatula to cut the bloomed gelatin in the mixer bowl into small pieces. When the syrup has cooled to 100°C (212°F), pour it over the gelatin and stir until the gelatin is melted. Place the bowl in the mixer, and whip with the whisk attachment for 1 minute on low speed. Increase the speed to high, and whip for about 5 minutes, until the mixture is very fluffy and begins to hold its shape. Stop the mixer, and add the vanilla extract, coconut and macadamia nuts. Whip on low until incorporated, about 30 seconds.

● Working quickly, fill a piping bag with the marshmallow mixture. Pipe into the moulds, which have already been coated with chocolate, leaving the top 3 mm (⅛ inch) of the cavity empty. Let set overnight.

● Use a ladle to pour the tempered milk chocolate into one mould at a time, over the set marshmallow fillings. Spread with a large offset spatula to completely cover the backs of the marshmallows. Let set. Flip the moulds over onto parchment paper, and tap the edges with the handle of an offset spatula to release the coconut shells. Store in an airtight container.

Tip: *If you don't have any moulds, these coconut marshmallows are delicious plain or dipped in chocolate according to the instructions on page 27.*

YOU WILL NEED

5 chocolate moulds with eight 5.5 cm (2¼-inch)-wide demi-sphere cavities

Narrow silicone brush

Wide silicone brush

Offset spatula

5-L (5-quart) stand mixer with whisk attachment

Fork

3-L (3-quart) saucepan

Heatproof silicone spatula

Pastry brush

Candy thermometer

Piping bag

Ladle

Parchment paper

115 g (4 ounces) dark chocolate, tempered (page 20) or melting chocolate

900 g (2 pounds) milk chocolate, tempered or coating chocolate, melted

3 tbsp (3 envelopes) unflavoured gelatin

180 ml (¾ cup) cold water

240 ml (1 cup) water

650 g (3¼ cups) sugar

½ teaspoon cream of tartar

⅛ teaspoon kosher salt

¼ teaspoon vanilla extract (page 130)

280 g (2 cups) finely shredded dried coconut

½ cup roasted macadamia nuts, finely chopped

450 g (1 pound) milk chocolate, tempered

Pastel Butter Mints

MAKES ABOUT 550 *g* ($1^1/_4$ *pound*)

Soft and melt-in-your-mouth creamy, these mints are perfectly refreshing.

YOU WILL NEED

Baking tray

Parchment paper

5-L (5-quart) stand mixer

Food-safe gloves

Chef's knife

METHOD

● Line a baking tray with parchment paper.

● Place the powdered sugar, cream, butter and mint extract in the bowl of a stand mixer. Beat on low with a paddle attachment until thoroughly combined. Increase the speed to medium, and beat until the mixture clumps around the paddle.

● Divide the resulting "dough" into batches, one batch for each colour of mint you're making. Apply drops of food colouring to each batch, aiming for pastel colours. Knead one batch with gloved hands, until the colour is uniform. Wash the gloves, and repeat for each batch.

● Roll the dough into 1-cm (½-inch)-wide ropes, and then cut each rope into 1-cm (½-inch)-long pieces. Arrange the pieces on the prepared baking tray so they don't touch each other. Let sit out uncovered overnight to dry. Store in an airtight container.

Tip: *Dividing the dough before you add the colouring allows you to make multiple colours from one batch. Without food colouring, the mints will be a light cream colour.*

540 g (4¾ cups) powdered sugar

2 tablespoons cream

115 g (½ cup) butter, softened

1 teaspoon mint extract

Food colouring as desired, 6 to 8 drops

Sweets Essentials
In the Pantry

We've talked about the luscious, silken, delicately crunchy and all-around incredible qualities of chocolate and sugar – they manifest beautiful creations and are the kings and queens of the sweets world. But what about the unsung heroes of sweetmaking? Peanut Brittle wouldn't be its delightful self without the peanuts. And billowy, cloud-like Vanilla Marshmallows simply wouldn't *be* if it weren't for vanilla extract. The following recipes will help you stock your pantry with flavours and garnishes essential to sweetmaking, and they may just infuse your imagination with taste inventions of your own!

Vanilla Extract

MAKES 1 L (1 quart)

It's very easy to make vanilla extract at home – and it's so good!
Try using a combination of different kinds of vanilla for a flavour that's
uniquely your own. Decanted into a decorative bottle, this homemade
vanilla makes a very special gift.

METHOD

● In a 1-L (1-quart) glass jar, mix together the brandy, vodka, vanilla
pods and seeds and vanilla extract, if using. Place the lid on the jar, and
let the mixture sit in a cool, dark place. It needs to sit for 3 months; add
used vanilla beans from baking, as available. Decant 120 ml (4 ounces)
of the vanilla extract into a small, decorative bottle, and top up the jar
with fresh brandy or vodka – the extract will last indefinitely this way.

Tip: *The optional vanilla extract in this recipe helps boost the flavour*
quickly, but it's not required.

1-L (1-quart) glass jar
with lid

400 ml (1⅔ cup) brandy

400 ml (1⅔ cup) vodka

5 vanilla beans, Tahitian
or Bourbon, split and
seeds scraped

85 g (3 ounces) vanilla
extract, Tahitian or
Bourbon (optional)

Vanilla extract adds
a sweet flavour to these
meringues (page 54).

Crystallised Citrus Peel

MAKES ABOUT 250 g (9 ounces)

This ingredient is deliciously versatile. A treat on its own or dipped in chocolate, crystallised citrus peel can also serve as an accent on top of or mixed into another type of sweets, such as nougat or caramel.

YOU WILL NEED

Paring knife

3-quart saucepan

Sieve

3 oranges, 5 lemons, or 2 grapefruits

2 cups water

2 cups sugar

¼ cup corn syrup or ¼ teaspoon cream of tartar

Pinch kosher salt

● With a paring knife, cut a thin slice off the tops and bottoms of each piece of fruit. Score the peel in 2.5-cm (1-inch)-wide strips, cutting just through the pith. Use your fingers to carefully peel off the strips of citrus peel.

● Place the peels in a 3-L (3-quart) saucepan, and add water to cover. Bring to a boil over medium-high heat, and then reduce the heat so the mixture gently simmers. Let cook 20 minutes, until tender. Drain the peels in a sieve.

● If the peels and piths are thicker than 5 mm (¼ inch), use a paring knife or spoon to scrape away the pith until the strips are 5 mm (¼ inch) thick. Cut the peels lengthwise into 5-mm (¼-inch) strips.

● In the saucepan, combine the water, sugar, corn syrup or cream of tartar and salt. Bring to a boil over medium-high heat. Add the trimmed citrus peel, and reduce the heat to low, so the mixture gently simmers. Cook until the peel is completely translucent and tender, about 30 to 45 minutes. Remove from the heat, and pour the peels and syrup into a heatproof container. Let sit overnight at room temperature, and then store the peel in its cooking syrup in the refrigerator.

● To cover the peel in sugar, remove the peel from syrup, and let it dry out overnight before rolling in granulated sugar.

Roasted Nuts

MAKES 450 g (*1 pound*)

Applying a "low and slow" cooking method to nuts enhances their flavour compared to toasting them at a high temperature for a short time. They also cook more evenly and are less likely to scorch. You can roast any amount of nuts at a time, but they will last for a while so larger batches are a good idea.

YOU WILL NEED

Baking tray

Parchment paper or silicone mat

450 g (1 pound) nuts, such as almonds, pecans, walnuts, pistachios

METHOD

● Preheat the oven to 121°C (250°F).

● Line a baking tray with parchment paper or a silicone mat. Spread out the nuts on the baking tray so that they are in a single layer. If roasting more than one kind of nut, keep them separate, and check that each is cooked separately, since they cook at different rates. Walnuts, for example, will be done in about 30 minutes while almonds will take about 60 minutes. Roast until they are evenly browned inside, stirring every 20 minutes.

Crystallised Ginger

MAKES ABOUT 450 g (1 pound)

For the most tender and flavourful results, be sure to use young, juicy and non-fibrous pieces of fresh ginger.

→ YOU WILL NEED

METHOD

● Place a cooling rack on a piece of parchment paper.

● Peel the ginger with a vegetable peeler or the edge of a spoon, and cut it into coin-shaped slices, 3-mm (⅛-inch) thick. Boil ginger and water, covered, over medium-high heat in a 3-L (3-quart) saucepan until the ginger is tender, about 40 minutes. Measure out 60 ml (¼ cup) of the ginger liquid and reserve. Drain the ginger, and then return it to the pot.

● Add the sugar and the reserved ginger liquid, and bring it to a boil over medium-high heat. Reduce the heat to medium, and stir the syrup frequently with a heatproof spatula until it boils away and the sugar begins to re-crystallise. Immediately remove the saucepan from the heat, and transfer the ginger to the cooling rack. Spread the ginger out with the spatula, and separate into individual pieces. Let cool, and store in an airtight container.

YOU WILL NEED

Cooling rack

Parchment paper

Vegetable peeler or spoon

Chef's knife

3-L (3-quart) saucepan

Strainer

Heatproof spatula

450 g (1 pound) fresh ginger

960 ml (4 cups) water

500 g (2½ cups) sugar

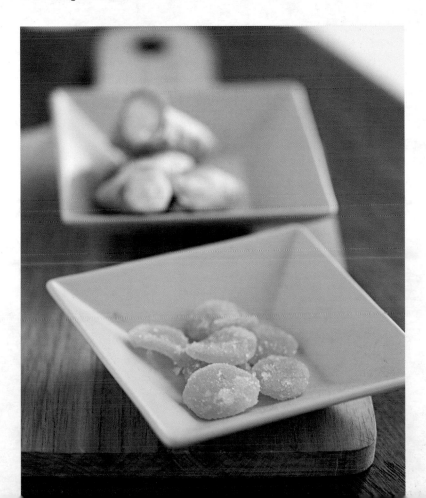

Acknowledgements

First and foremost, I'd like to thank my family, especially my mum and dad, who taught me that the only thing better than eating good food is to share it. I'd also like to thank Carolyn Wong, owner of Carolyn Wong Cakes, whose taste buds and suggestions were invaluable in the creation of this collection of recipes.

I'd like to thank everyone at Lark, especially Beth Sweet and Kristi Pfeffer, for their editorial and creative support of all things sweets. Deep gratitude is offered to the amazing White on Rice Couple, Todd Porter and Diane Cu, for capturing these gorgeous photos. Many thanks to Kathy Sheldon, for lending her copyediting finesse to these pages, and appreciation goes to Eileen Paulin and Erika Kotite.

Warm thanks to all of those who have influenced, helped, taught and generally enlivened me during my sweetmaking adventures. Both this cookbook and my company, BonBonBar Confections, have benefited from so much kind encouragement and generosity. Thanks to: Annie Baker, Matt Bercovitz, Chad Boyda, Michael Boyda, CJ Calvert, The Candy Store (Diane, Brian, and Liana), Jun Chen, Tania Clucas, Stephen Durfee, Evelyn FitzGibbon, Foodzie, Clemence Gossett, Joyce Guan, Clarine Lim Hardesty, Marie and Darrell Jackson, Jodi Koenig, Dafna Kory, Susannah Lescher, Pouneh Rajaii, Marika Shimamoto-Doob, Chuck Siegel, Jeri Sisco, Anastasia Widiarsih and Bonnie Yu.

About the Author

Nina Wanat was born in Brooklyn, New York, and raised in New Jersey. She initially moved to California for the film industry, but she stayed for the food. After dropping out of law school, she studied baking and pastry at the Culinary Institute of America at Greystone and apprenticed with artisan chocolatiers. In 2007, she founded BonBonBar Confections, which specialises in handmade sweets bars, caramels and marshmallows. She lives in San Francisco.

METRIC CONVERSION CHART BY VOLUME
(for Liquids)

U.S.	Metric (milliliters/liters)
¼ teaspoon	1.25 mL
½ teaspoon	2.5 mL
1 teaspoon	5 mL
1 tablespoon	15 mL
¼ cup	60 mL
½ cup	120 mL
¾ cup	180 mL
1 cup	240 mL
2 cups (1 pint)	480 mL
4 cups (1 quart)	960 mL
4 quarts (1 gallon)	3.8 L

METRIC CONVERSION CHART BY WEIGHT
(for Dry Ingredients)

U.S.	Metric (grams/kilograms)
¼ teaspoon	1 g
½ teaspoon	2 g
1 teaspoon	5 g
1 tablespoon	15 g
16 ounces (1 pound)	450 g
2 pounds	900 g
3 pounds	1.4 kg
4 pounds	1.8 kg
5 pounds	2.3 kg
6 pounds	2.7 kg

COOKING MEASUREMENT EQUIVALENTS

3 teaspoons = 1 tablespoon
2 tablespoons = 1 fluid ounce
4 tablespoons = ¼ cup
5 tablespoons + 1 teaspoon = ⅓ cup
8 tablespoons = ½ cup
10 tablespoons + 2 teaspoons = ⅔ cup
12 tablespoons = ¾ cup
16 tablespoons = 1 cup
48 teaspoons = 1 cup
1 cup = 8 fluid ounces
2 cups = 1 pint
2 pints = 1 quart
4 quarts = 1 gallon

TEMPERATURE CONVERSION

Fahrenheit	Celsius
32°	0°
212°	100°
250°	121°
275°	135°
300°	149°
350°	177°
375°	191°
400°	204°
425°	218°

METRIC CONVERSIONS

Index